Demystifying Azure AI

Implementing the Right AI Features for Your Business

Kasam Shaikh

Apress®

Demystifying Azure AI: Implementing the Right AI Features for Your Business

Kasam Shaikh
Kalyan, Maharashtra, India

ISBN-13 (pbk): 978-1-4842-6218-4   ISBN-13 (electronic): 978-1-4842-6219-1
https://doi.org/10.1007/978-1-4842-6219-1

Managing Director, Apress Media LLC: Welmoed Spahr
Acquisitions Editor: Smriti Srivastava
Development Editor: Laura Berendson
Coordinating Editor: Shrikant Vishwakarma

Cover designed by eStudioCalamar

Cover image designed by Freepik (www.freepik.com)

Distributed to the book trade worldwide by Springer Science+Business Media New York, 233 Spring Street, 6th Floor, New York, NY 10013. Phone 1-800-SPRINGER, fax (201) 348-4505, e-mail orders-ny@springer-sbm.com, or visit www.springeronline.com. Apress Media, LLC is a California LLC and the sole member (owner) is Springer Science + Business Media Finance Inc (SSBM Finance Inc). SSBM Finance Inc is a **Delaware** corporation.

For information on translations, please e-mail booktranslations@springernature.com; for reprint, paperback, or audio rights, please e-mail bookpermissions@springernature.com.

Apress titles may be purchased in bulk for academic, corporate, or promotional use. eBook versions and licenses are also available for most titles. For more information, reference our Print and eBook Bulk Sales web page at http://www.apress.com/bulk-sales.

Any source code or other supplementary material referenced by the author in this book is available to readers on GitHub via the book's product page, located at www.apress.com/978-1-4842-6218-4. For more detailed information, please visit http://www.apress.com/source-code.

Printed on acid-free paper

This book is dedicated to my father, the late Mr. Ahmed Kasam Shaikh, who is always a source of inspiration for me. And to my mentor, Mr. Sabarinath Iyer.

Table of Contents

About the Author

Kasam Shaikh, cloud advocate, is a seasoned professional with 13 years of demonstrated industry experience working as a cloud architect with one of the leading IT companies in Mumbai, India. He is recognized as an MVP by an online tech community, and he is also a global Azure AI speaker, and author of two best-selling books on Microsoft Azure and AI. He is the founder of the Azure INDIA (az-INDIA) community, and Dear Azure, an online community for learning Azure AI. He owns a YouTube channel and shares his experience at his website, https://www.kasamshaikh.com.

About the Technical Reviewer

 **Adwait Churi** is a seasoned professional, an AI speaker, reviewer, and trainer, with a keen interested in cloud technologies. He has more than 13 years of software industry experience in team building, training, development, support, and Agile practices. He is a Center Of Excellence member with Cloud Research and Development and has architected business-critical applications in the banking, financial services, and insurance fields, as well as learning management systems, health care, and hospitality domains.

He is passionate about advancing technologies including cloud, integration, microservices, securities, Extract-Transform-Load, and Dev-Ops.

His day-to-day work helps organizations in software application architecture and designing, presales, performance engineering, project management, and software development.

Adwait provides training courses on Microsoft BizTalk Server, MuleSoft, and Microsoft Azure. He can be reached on LinkedIn at www.linkedin.com/in/adwait-churi-b079a1106 or on Twitter at @adwaitchuri.

Acknowledgments

First, I would like to thank Almighty ALLAH, my mother, and especially my better half for motivating me throughout the process. I would also like to thank Mandar Dharmadhikari for his continuous support and providing his valuable knowledge about modern integration workflows.

I am highly thankful to Apress for believing in me and trusting me with this opportunity.

CHAPTER 1

Working with Azure Cognitive Search

I would like congratulate you for starting with the toughest part of learning: starting! The fact that you are reading this book means you have taken the very first step to begin learning. I will ensure that this learning journey of Microsoft Azure AI will be a beneficial one. In this first chapter, I will introduce the recent most powerful service offered by Microsoft Azure for AI with cloud search, Azure Cognitive Search.

Introduction to Azure Cognitive Search

Azure Cognitive Search is a cloud search service powered by artificial intelligence (AI) for mobile, web, or your inline business application development. Formerly known as Azure Search, this the only cloud search service that transforms your unstructured data into an identifiable, searchable format with its built-in AI capabilities, saving lots of time for an organization building a complex search solution.

Approximately 83 percent of organizations have their data in unstructured, nonmaintainable formats. Later they must invest resources in developing a data search system. Azure Cognitive Search helps enrich these unstructured data stored in the form of PDF documents, images, word processing documents, and so on, into a structured, indexed, ready-to-search format.

© Kasam Shaikh 2020
K. Shaikh, *Demystifying Azure AI*, https://doi.org/10.1007/978-1-4842-6219-1_1

Here are few notable features of Azure Cognitive Search.

- Fully managed search as a service to ease the complexity and scale effortlessly.

- Autocomplete, geospatial search, filtering, and faceting capabilities for a rich user experience

- Built-in AI capabilities including optical character recognition (OCR), key phrase extraction, and named entity recognition.

- Seamless integration of custom models, classifiers, and rankers to fit your domain-specific requirements.

It is important to note that when I say search on cloud, that doesn't mean search all of the data on the cloud, but your data on the cloud. This means data you provide to the service to enrich it with AI cognitive and custom AI skills, to make it presentable. It follows a simple pattern, as shown in Figure 1-1.

***Figure 1-1.** Service pattern view*

- **Ingest:** The unstructured data in any format to be seeded to Azure Cognitive Search by any Azure Store.

- **Enrich:** Cognitive skills or custom skills are applied to the data.

- **Explore:** A searchable data set is ready to explore.

Before I start with the exercise of creating this service, let's cover this pattern in more detail.

Ingest

In this phase, the unstructured data are provided to Azure Cognitive Search from an available Azure Store. The following data formats are supported:

- `.pdf, .rtf, .doc`
- `.jpg, .xml, .json`
- `.ppt, .tif, .png`
- `.html, .xls, .bmp`

These are the available data sources:

- Blob storage
- Azure SQL
- Cosmos DB
- Azure tables
- MySQL
- Azure Files
- ADLS Gen2

Figure 1-2 defines the ingest form.

Figure 1-2. Ingest form in pattern

Note   These formats and sources are available at the time of writing. More formats and sources could be added in the near future.

Document cracking takes place here once seeded. It converts the unstructured data into text, images, and metadata. These data are then passed to Cognitive Services for further enrichment as required. This is explained visually in Figure 1-3.

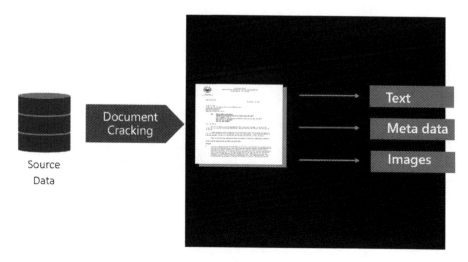

Figure 1-3. *Document cracking explained*

Enrich

This is the most important phase of applying cognitive or custom skills to the data (Figure 1-4). You can apply a set of Azure Cognitive Services to data to transform it into smart, searchable output. This is the same integrated cognitive stack that has been used by Microsoft Bing and Microsoft Office for more than a decade and is used for AI services across vision, language, and speech.

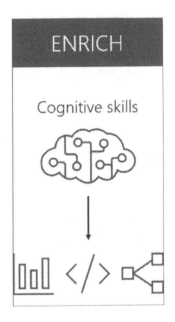

Figure 1-4. Enrichment form in pattern

Some of the cutting-edge AI services that are added for enrichment are listed in Table 1-1.

Table 1-1. Azure Cognitive Services

AI Skills	Azure Cognitive Service	Performs Action
Key phrase extraction	Text Analytics	Returns a list of key phrases from unstructured data
Organization entity extraction	Entity Recognition	Returns "Organization" entity category
Location entity extraction	Entity Recognition	Returns "Location" entity category from unstructured data

(continued)

Table 1-1. (*continued*)

AI Skills	Azure Cognitive Service	Performs Action
Person entity extraction	Entity Recognition	Returns "Organization" entity category from unstructured data
Landmark detection	Computer Vision	Returns landmark details from unstructured data
Language detection	Text Analytics	Returns language details
Celebrity recognition	Computer Vision	Returns with celebrity details if recognized from the data
Sentiment analysis	Text Analytics	Returns sentiments of the data content
Face detection	Facial Recognition	Returns facial details
Tag extraction	Text Analytics	Extracts tags from the data
Printed text recognition	OCR	Read the text from images
Custom skills	All Azure Cognitive Services	

Figure 1-5 presents the overall flow of this pattern, on applying AI skills to enrich the data ingested into the service.

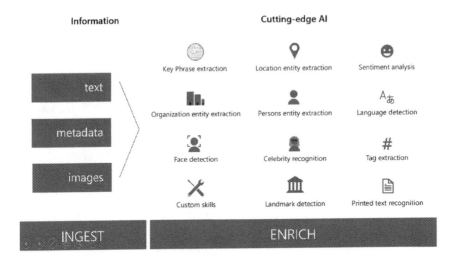

Figure 1-5. *Enrich ingested data with Azure Cognitive Services*

Now, even the images resulting from document cracking on ingested data can be further refined to extract printed text on images, face detection, object detection, and so on, and added as the part of text for further fnrichment skill sets. You can also add custom skills to the merged text. An enriched sample skill set is presented in Figure 1-6.

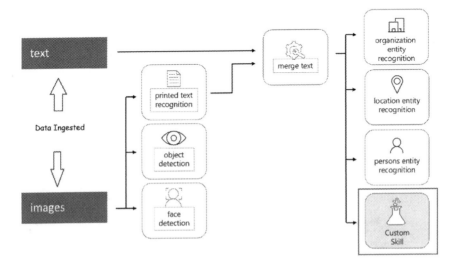

Figure 1-6. *View of enriched sample skill set*

Note   You can add custom skills and empower more refinement of data. This is not covered in this book.

Explore

Finally, after ingest and enrich, the unstructured data are now ready for the explore phase. The data are now available for search operations like full-text search, highlighted text search, filter, facet, and many more smart forms of search operations.

The complete pattern is shown in Figure 1-7.

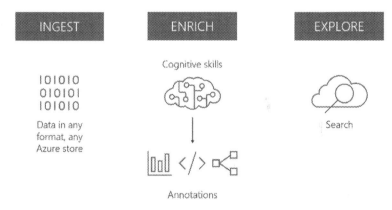

Figure 1-7. *Pattern of Azure Cognitive Search*

The pattern flow can be a bit confusing, but it is clearer in graphic format. Now that I have introduced the way it works, we can explore the pattern flow in action. I will introduce new terms and concepts as we encounter them.

Creating Azure Cognitive Search

Let's get started with the service. Throughout the book, I will be using Azure Management Portal for the exercises to make your reading easier. You can explore the other available methods on your own, like REST application programming interfaces (APIs), software development kits (SDKs), Azure Resource Manager (ARM), or Powershell.

Prerequisites

For all the exercises, you need a valid Azure subscription. You can also create a free Azure account for a one-month trial to explore the offerings of Azure.

Assuming you have a valid Azure subscription, let's start working with Azure Cognitive Search. Open Azure Management Portal, (`https://portal.azure.com`) and click Create A New Resource either on the home screen or the left menu (Figure 1-8).

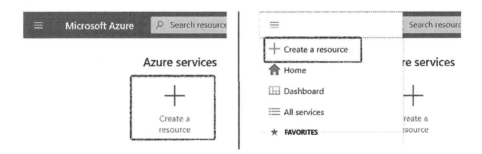

Figure 1-8. *Starting creation of an Azure resource*

Enter Azure Cognitive Search in the search bar and click Search. This will open the service window. Click Create to proceed, as shown in Figure 1-9.

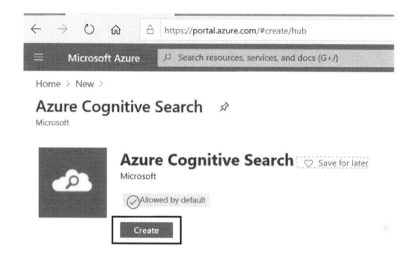

Figure 1-9. *Azure Cognitive Service resource page*

You will see a blade with several tabs to fill in with details.

On the Basics tab, you need to provide basic details like name, resource group, location, and pricing tier, all of which are mandatory to proceed with further sections. Provide the following details.

- *Subscription:* Provide your valid subscription here.

- *Resource Group:* – You can create a new group or use the existing resource group.

- *URL:* You can use any available name, which will later be part of the Search API URL; for example, `https://<servicename>.search.window.net`.

- *Location:* Location of your choice.

- *Pricing Tier: Select the appropriate* tier from the available pricing tiers. I will use the Free tier here (Figure 1-10), to present you with all the capabilities you can leverage at no cost.

Select Pricing Tier
Browse available skus and their features

Sku	Offering	Indexes	Indexers	Storage	Search units	Replicas	Partitions	Cost/month (estimated)
F	Free	3	3	50 MB	1	1	1	₹0.00
B	Basic	15	15	2 GB	3	3	1	₹4,966.74
S	Standard	50	50	25 GB/Partition*	36	12	12	₹16,523.00
S2	Standard	200	200	100 GB/Partition*	36	12	12	₹66,092.02
S3	Standard	200	200	200 GB/Partition*	36	12	12	₹132,184.04
S3HD	High-density	1000	0	200 GB/Partition*	36	12	3	₹132,184.04
L1	Storage Optimized	10	10	1 TB/Partition*	36	12	12	₹188,785.17
L2	Storage Optimized	10	10	2 TB/Partition*	36	12	12	₹377,521.16

Figure 1-10. *Current available pricing tiers*

Once you have filled in all the details on the Basics tab (Figure 1-11),
click the Scale tab.

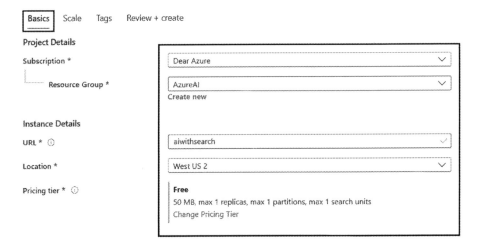

Figure 1-11. *Details provided on the Basics tab*

The Scale tab includes settings to create the following elements, as
shown in Figure 1-12.

- *Replicas:* Replicas distribute workloads across the service.

- *Partitions:* Partitions allow for scaling of document
  count (this applies to Standard and Storage Optimized
  tiers only).

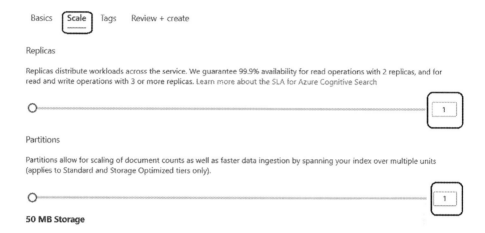

Figure 1-12. *Settings on the Scale tab*

Leave the default selections as they are. Click Tags to open the next tab.

The settings on the Tags tab are not mandatory, but it is advisable to provide these details for easy resource management. You can set tags, as shown in Figure 1-13, and then click Next to proceed with the validation.

Figure 1-13. *Details provided on the Tags tab*

Finally click the Review + Create tab to complete the resource provisioning process. with the first element on this tab is the validation. If there are any issues, it will stop and notify you; if all is good to proceed, it displays the message Validation Success, as shown in Figure 1-14.

Figure 1-14. *Review + Create tab with a validation message and Create button*

You can review the details here. If you need to change any details, click Previous to return to earlier tabs.

Note   When you opt for a pricing tier higher than Free (i.e., Basic and higher), you are presented with one more tab, Networking, which allows you to set the service endpoints to be public or private (Figure 1-15). Because we are using the Free tier, the Networking tab was hidden.

Figure 1-15. *Networking tab*

When your tabs are set, click Create to start provisioning. Once it is deployed, open the resource page, displayed in Figure 1-16.

Figure 1-16. *Azure Cognitive Search resource overview page*

Notice the settings for service URL, location and service status. Also, as I have opted for the Free tier, Storage of 50 MB and a maximum quota of 3 for Indexes and Indexers are presented in Figure 1-16.

Now that the the service is created, let's start with first step, to ingest the data.

Ingest

I have the minimum set storage and index quota assigned with the Free tier. For further steps in this exercise, we will use with the sample data provided by Microsoft Azure to import to the service. You could also select the available data sources like Azure Blob or Azure SQL using the Free tier, but using the sample data will give a better picture of how things work more efficiently.

To proceed, click Import Data, as highlighted in Figure 1-16. The Import Data page will present you with the several tabs.

On the Connect to Your Data tab, you will create and load a search index using data from an existing Azure data source from your subscription or from the sample data (Figure 1-17). Theoretically, an index is similar to a table, and documents are roughly equivalent to rows in a table. Any document we upload is a single unit of searchable data in an index. You can directly create an index from Azure Portal or REST APIs, or can upload the data, and then set an index from the identified fields. Azure Cognitive Search crawls the data structure you provide, extracts searchable content, optionally enriches it with cognitive skills, and loads it into an index.

Import data

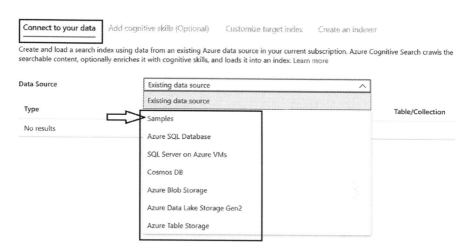

Figure 1-17. *List of data sources available to connect data to Azure Cognitive Search*

If you select any other source apart from Samples, you need to provide additional details with respect to the source selected. For example, if you select Azure Blob Storage, you need to provide details like the default connection string, container name, and specific blob, if any. Figure 1-18 provides and example of the available options in this case.

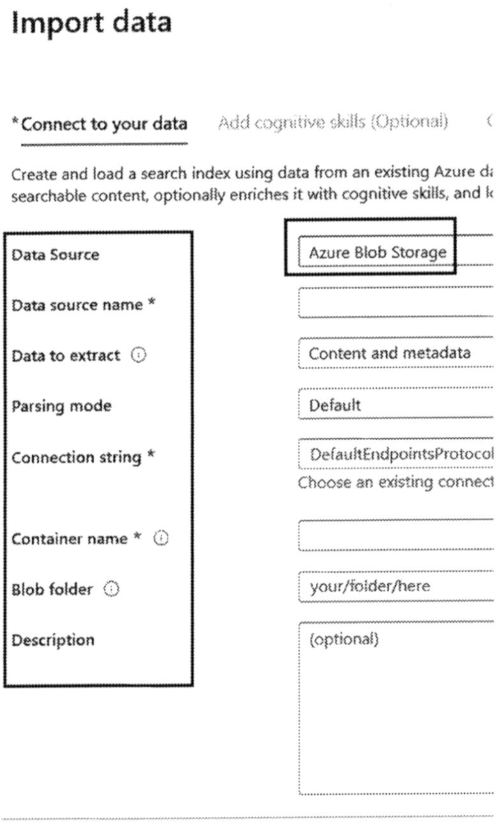

Import data

*Connect to your data   Add cognitive skills (Optional)

Create and load a search index using data from an existing Azure d;
searchable content, optionally enriches it with cognitive skills, and l

Data Source	Azure Blob Storage
Data source name *	
Data to extract ⓘ	Content and metadata
Parsing mode	Default
Connection string *	DefaultEndpointsProtocol
	Choose an existing connect
Container name * ⓘ	
Blob folder ⓘ	your/folder/here
Description	(optional)

Figure 1-18. *Azure Blob Storage details required to connect data to Azure Cognitive Search*

Similarly, you will need to present different details depending on the data source selected.

Once you have selected Samples for this exercise, you will see another two options to be selected as your data, as shown in Figure 1-19.

- *Azure SQL Database:* This has sample data related to a real estate domain.

- *Azure Cosmos DB:* This has sample data related to hotels.

Data Source	Samples	⌄

Type	Name
🏠	realestate-us-sample
✈	hotels-sample

Figure 1-19. *Available sample data*

For this exercise, I have selected the Azure SQL database for this
exercise, but you can use the Azure Cosmos DB if you wish to.

Note   At the time of writing, these are the only two options in
Samples. This could change in the future.

You will not be asked for any further details related to the Azure
SQL database or Azure Cosmos DB as mentioned earlier, as these data
are presented by Microsoft Azure as samples, and include all relevant
information.

Select the required database—in my case the Azure SQL database—
and move on to the next tab by clicking the button at bottom of the page.
Once clicked, it will validate and proceed further, presenting the next tab
to add cognitive skills. This is where the data enrichment will take place.

As shown in Figure 1-20, the Add Cognitive Skills (Optional) tab
provides three actions to perform.

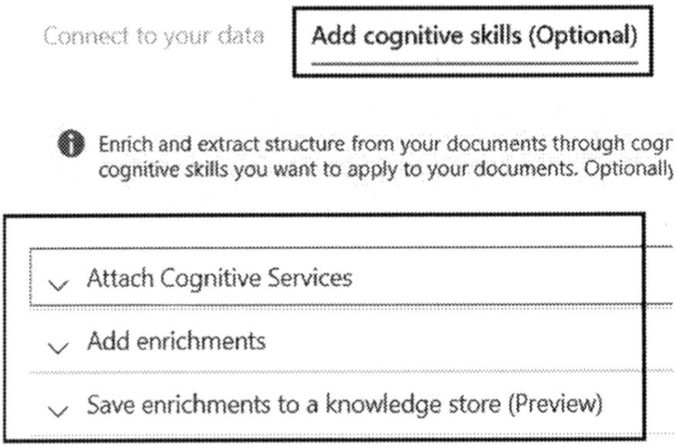

Connect to your data   **Add cognitive skills (Optional)**

ℹ Enrich and extract structure from your documents through cogn
cognitive skills you want to apply to your documents. Optionally

∨ Attach Cognitive Services

∨ Add enrichments

∨ Save enrichments to a knowledge store (Preview)

Figure 1-20. *Add Cognitive Skills (Optional) tab settings for data enrichment*

- *Attach Cognitive Services:* As the name suggests, to leverage cognitive skills, here you need to select an existing Cognitive Services resource or create a new one. An important point to remember here is that the Cognitive Services resource should be in the same region as your Azure Cognitive Search service.

Note   The execution of cognitive skills will be billed to the selected resource. Otherwise, the number of enrichments executions will be limited.

Here you also have an option to select the free cognitive service resource, which comes with limited enrichments. Let's create a new cognitive service resource here, and attach the same.

Either enter Cognitive Services in the search box at the top of the screen, or click Create New Cognitive Services Resources at the bottom of the section, as highlighted in Figure 1-21.

Figure 1-21. *Attach Cognitive Services settings*

Clicking that link opens a new window to create a resource with all cognitive services, as shown in Figure 1-22. You need to provide the following details.

- *Name:* Service name of your choice.

- *Subscription:* Your valid subscription.

- *Location:* Location that is the same as the location of the Azure cognitive service you are working with.

- *Pricing Tier:* You can go minimum with the Standard tier. For details on pricing, visit `https://azure.microsoft.com/en-in/pricing/details/cognitive-services/`.

- *Resource Group:* Select the resource group with which you want to group the service.

- *Agree with notice:* Read the notice presented by Microsoft with respect to usage of data carefully. If you agree, select the corresponding check box.

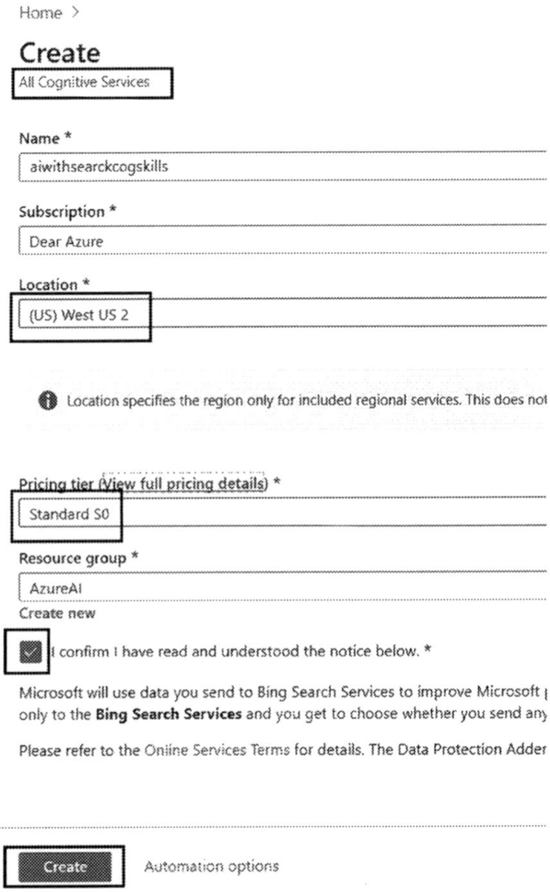

Home >

Create

All Cognitive Services

Name *

aiwithsearckcogskills

Subscription *

Dear Azure

Location *

(US) West US 2

ℹ Location specifies the region only for included regional services. This does not

Pricing tier (View full pricing details) *

Standard S0

Resource group *

AzureAI

Create new

☑ I confirm I have read and understood the notice below. *

Microsoft will use data you send to Bing Search Services to improve Microsoft
only to the **Bing Search Services** and you get to choose whether you send any

Please refer to the Online Services Terms for details. The Data Protection Adder

Create   Automation options

Figure 1-22. *Window to create Cognitive Services*

Click Create to proceed with validation and creation of a Cognitive
Services resource. To verify, open the Cognitive Services window,
displayed in Figure 1-23, once the resource is created.

Figure 1-23. *Cognitive resource overview page*

Click Refresh, as shown in Figure 1-21, to see this newly created cognitive service listed in the Attach section. Attach it by selecting the newly created service, as shown in Figure 1-24.

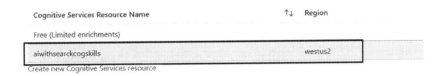

Figure 1-24. *The newly created cognitive service*

- *Add Enrichments:* In this section, you can select the cognitive skills to run on the imported data. For this example, displayed in Figure 1-25, I have selected all the available skills, along with setting the text translation target language to Arabic. You can also configure Skillset Name and the Source Data Field settings, listed from the imported data. I have selected the default values.

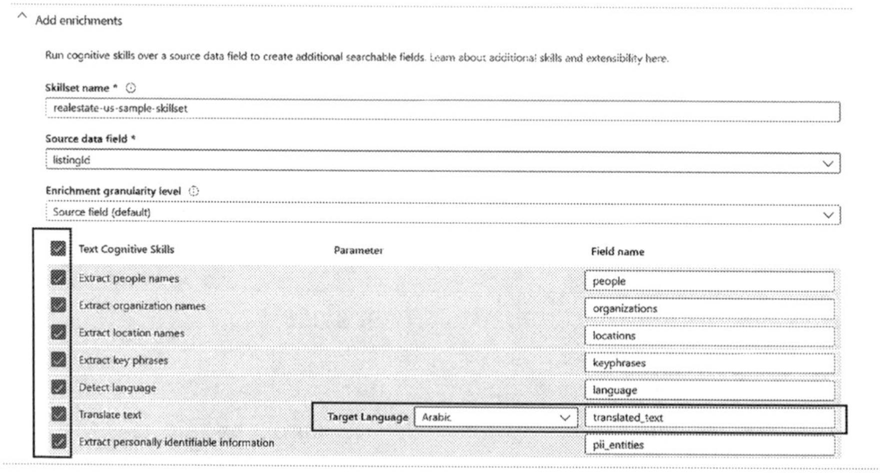

Figure 1-25. *Settings in the Add Enrichments section*

- *Save eEnrichments To A Knowledge Store (Preview):*
  This option is still in preview, where in you can save the
  enriched data like key phrases to Azure Blob. You can
  further visualize the data from knowledge store with
  Power BI. As this option is in preview, I do not cover
  this further in the chapter.

After going through all three (or two) options, click Next: Customize
Target Index to validate and proceed to the next section.

Here you can see all the fields listed based on cognitive skills you
added to the imported data. For instance, as I have selected the Arabic
language to translate the text, you can see the field added as translated_
text with Arabic (highlighted in Figure 1-26).

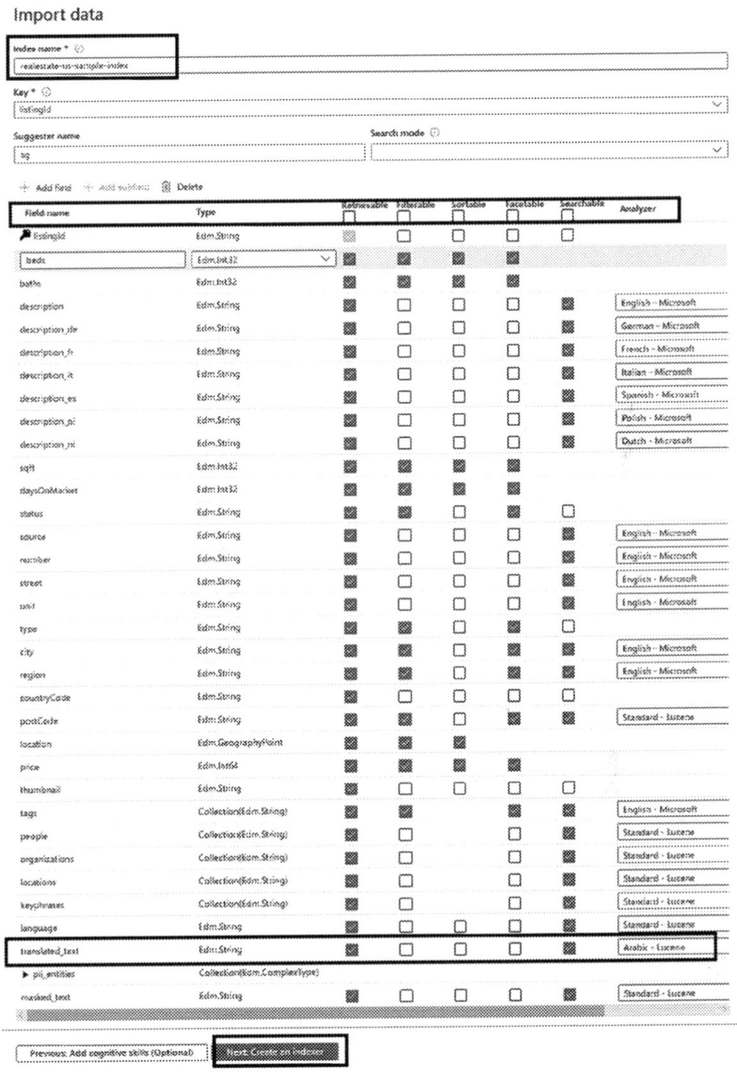

Import data

Index name *
realestate-us-sample-index

Key *
listingId

Suggester name
sg

Search mode

+ Add field   + Add subfield   ⊟ Delete

Field name	Type	Retrievable	Filterable	Sortable	Facetable	Searchable	Analyzer
listingId	Edm.String	■	☐	☐	☐	☐	
beds	Edm.Int32	■	■	■	■		
baths	Edm.Int32	■	■	■	■		
description	Edm.String	■	☐	☐	☐	■	English - Microsoft
description_de	Edm.String	■	☐	☐	☐	■	German – Microsoft
description_fr	Edm.String	■	☐	☐	☐	■	French – Microsoft
description_it	Edm.String	■	☐	☐	☐	■	Italian - Microsoft
description_es	Edm.String	■	☐	☐	☐	■	Spanish - Microsoft
description_pl	Edm.String	■	☐	☐	☐	■	Polish - Microsoft
description_nl	Edm.String	■	☐	☐	☐	■	Dutch - Microsoft
sqft	Edm.Int32	■	■	■	■		
daysOnMarket	Edm.Int32	■	■	■	■		
status	Edm.String	■	■	☐	■	☐	
source	Edm.String	■	☐	☐	☐	■	English - Microsoft
number	Edm.String	■	☐	☐	☐	■	English - Microsoft
street	Edm.String	■	☐	☐	☐	■	English - Microsoft
unit	Edm.String	■	☐	☐	☐	■	English - Microsoft
type	Edm.String	■	■	☐	■	☐	
city	Edm.String	■	■	☐	■	■	English - Microsoft
region	Edm.String	■	■	☐	■	■	English - Microsoft
countryCode	Edm.String	■	☐	☐	☐	☐	
postCode	Edm.String	■	■	☐	■	■	Standard - Lucene
location	Edm.GeographyPoint	■	■	■			
price	Edm.Int64	■	■	■	■		
thumbnail	Edm.String	■	☐	☐	☐	☐	
tags	Collection(Edm.String)	■	■		■	■	English - Microsoft
people	Collection(Edm.String)	■	☐		☐	■	Standard - Lucene
organizations	Collection(Edm.String)	■	☐		☐	■	Standard - Lucene
locations	Collection(Edm.String)	■	☐		☐	■	Standard - Lucene
keyphrases	Collection(Edm.String)	■	☐		☐	■	Standard - Lucene
language	Edm.String	■	☐	☐	☐	■	Standard - Lucene
translated_text	Edm.String	■	☐	☐	☐	■	Arabic - Lucene
▶ pii_entities	Collection(Edm.ComplexType)						
masked_text	Edm.String	■	☐	☐	☐	■	Standard - Lucene

Previous: Add cognitive skills (Optional)   Next: Create an indexer

Figure 1-26. *All the index fields listed based on the Enrichments section*

You can perform the following actions with the listed field.

- Add more fields to index.

- Remove a field from the list.

- Set the field to be retrievable.

- Set the field to be filterable.

- Set the field to be sortable.

- Set the field to be Facetable.

- Set the field to be searchable.

Once you have complete all the required actions just mentioned, click on the final tab to create an indexer.

An *indexer*, in the service, is a crawler that extracts searchable data and metadata from imported data and populates the given index based on field-to-field mappings between the index and your data source.

You can run indexers on demand or on a recurring data refresh schedule that runs as often as every five minutes.

Note   A schedule cannot be configured on samples or existing data sources without change tracking. Edit your data source to add change tracking if you wish to set up a schedule.

Click Submit, as shown in Figure 1-27, to complete the steps, validate, and create the indexer.

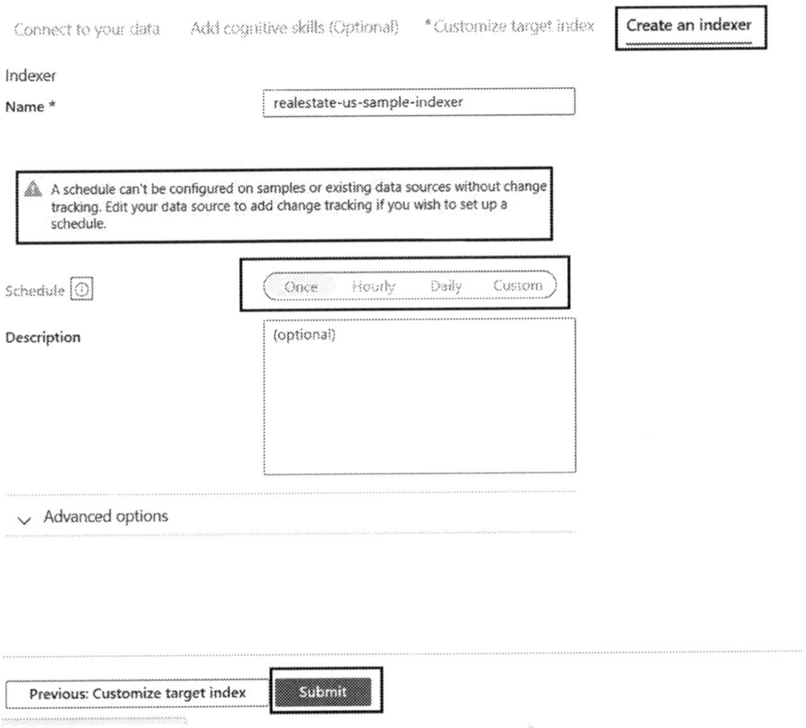

Connect to your data   Add cognitive skills (Optional)   * Customize target index   **Create an indexer**

Indexer

Name *

realestate-us-sample-indexer

⚠ A schedule can't be configured on samples or existing data sources without change tracking. Edit your data source to add change tracking if you wish to set up a schedule.

Schedule ⓘ

Once   Hourly   Daily   Custom

Description

(optional)

⌄ Advanced options

Previous: Customize target index   Submit

Figure 1-27. *Creating and setting an indexer schedule*

You can check the status of indexer creation in the Overview section on the Indexers tab (Figure 1-28).

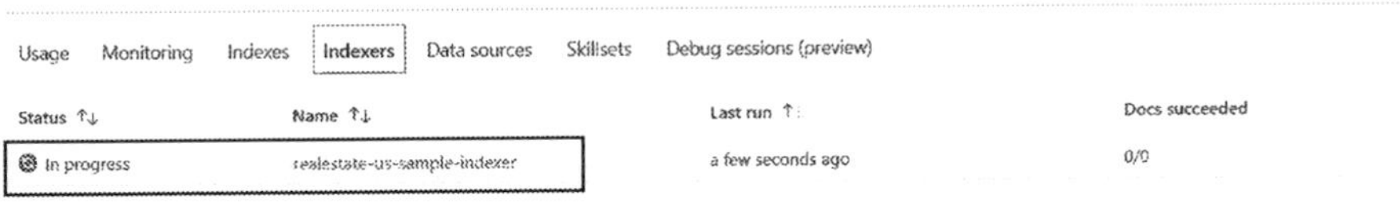

Usage	Monitoring	Indexes	Indexers	Data sources	Skillsets	Debug sessions (preview)	
Status ↑↓		Name ↑↓			Last run ↑		Docs succeeded
🔄 In progress		realestate-us-sample-indexer			a few seconds ago		0/0

Figure 1-28. *Checking status of creation of indexers*

Click Refresh at the top of the page to display the updated status.

The overview page for the services provides all the details we configured in the preceding steps,

- *Usage:* This tab, shown in Figure 1-29, displays storage usage by the imported data, in this case the sample database.

Figure 1-29. *Usage tab of the Overview section*

- *Monitoring:* On this tab, shown in Figure 1-30, you can monitor the nature of API calls made to the service.

Figure 1-30. *Monitoring tab of the Overview section*

- *Indexes:* This tab, displayed in Figure 1-31, shows the indexes added to a service.

Figure 1-31. *Indexes tab of the Overview section*

- *Indexers:* This tab, shown in Figure 1-32, shows indexers created for the unstructured imported data. The time taken and count of docs varies from data set to data set.

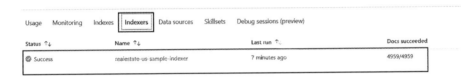

Figure 1-32. *Indexers tab of the Overview section*

- *Data Sources:* This tab, as displayed in Figure 1-33, shows sources added to a service to import data, in this case, the sample database.

Figure 1-33. *Data Sources tab of the Overview section*

- *Skillsets:* This tab, illustrated in Figure 1-34, includes the details of cognitive custom skills added as part of enrichment.

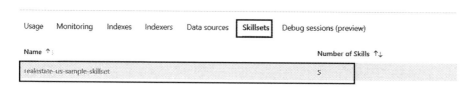

Figure 1-34. *Skillsets tab of the Overview section*

- *Debug Sessions (Preview):* This tab is in preview. It helps you debug your enrichment pipeline, especially when your indexers are generating errors or warnings. To view the overall status message, shown in Figure 1-35, go to the Indexers tab, and click the indexer name listed.

Figure 1-35. *Detailed view of indexers status*

You can again run or delete the indexers on this tab.

Search Explorer

Now it's time to explore search functions on the enriched data, the third and final part of our pattern.

Open the Indexes tab and click on the listed index on which you want to explore the search.

You will be taken to the appropriate page, presenting you with many options, along with Search Explorer. Here, in Figure 1-36, you can see all of the details with respect to storage size being used, along with the number of documents. You are presented with a text box for entering a query string, based on which the search will take place. Further, it displays the API version and a Request URL field, which changes based on values you add in the query string.

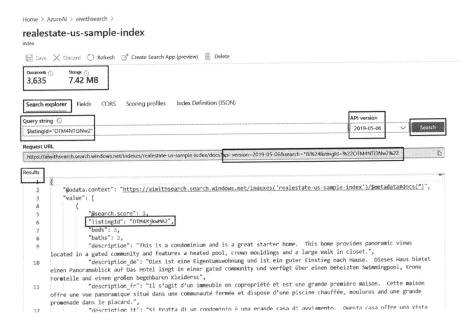

Figure 1-36. *Search Explorer view*

You can explore the other tabs like Fields, CORS, Scoring Profiles, and Index Definition (JSON) on your own.

Creating a Search App

Finally, you can create a search app based on this result. Earlier the code to create the app was provided via a link to a GitHub repo. Now it is available by clicking a button at the top of the Search Explorer page. This feature is available as a preview, as it is evolving with more advanced options, but I use this option here.

Click Create Search App (Preview) at the top of the window, as shown in Figure 1-37.

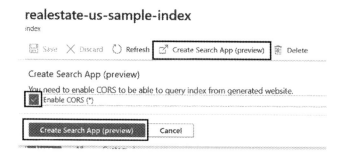

Figure 1-37. *Window prompting the user to enable CORS*

You will be prompted within the window to enable CORS, as you will be querying the index from the generated website. Select the Enable CORS check box, and click Create Search App (Preview).

You will then see three tabs, where you can indicate data to populate a website user interface (UI) layout.

- *Individual Result:* On this tab, shown in Figure 1-38, you can customize how individual results will be displayed. The layout corresponds to how each result will be rendered.

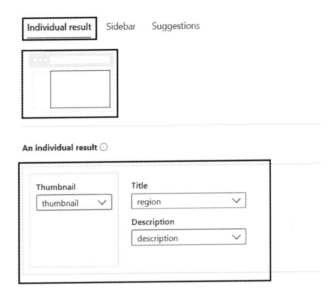

Figure 1-38. *UI component for an individual result*

- *Sidebar:* On this tab you can choose and customize filters that will be displayed in the sidebar (Figure 1-39). Only fields that are filterable and facetable can be used. The order of the table corresponds to the order in which the fields are displayed in the sidebar.

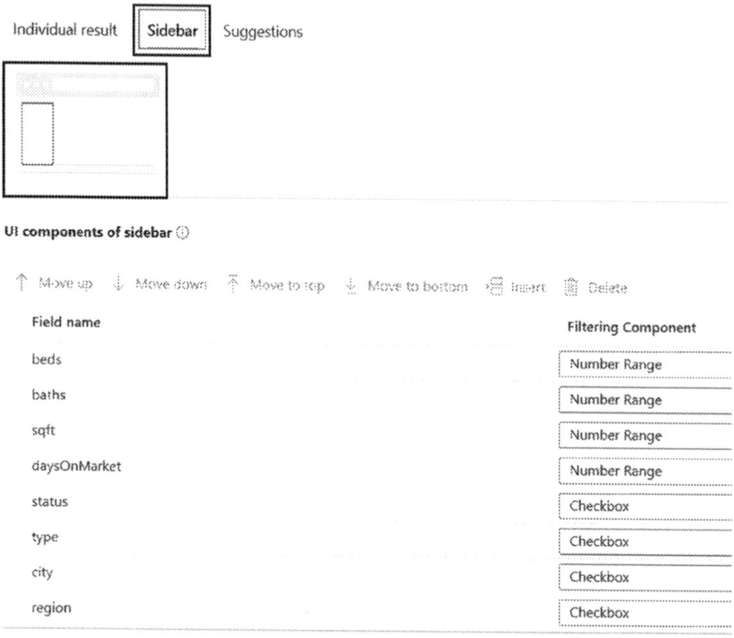

Individual result | **Sidebar** | Suggestions

UI components of sidebar ⓘ

↑ Move up   ↓ Move down   ⤒ Move to top   ⤓ Move to bottom   ⊟ Insert   🗑 Delete

Field name	Filtering Component
beds	Number Range
baths	Number Range
sqft	Number Range
daysOnMarket	Number Range
status	Checkbox
type	Checkbox
city	Checkbox
region	Checkbox

Figure 1-39. *UI component for sidebar*

- *Suggestion:* On this tab, shown in Figure 1-40, you can choose and customize which fields will be displayed as suggestions in the search box drop-down list. The order of the table corresponds to the order that the fields are displayed for each result.

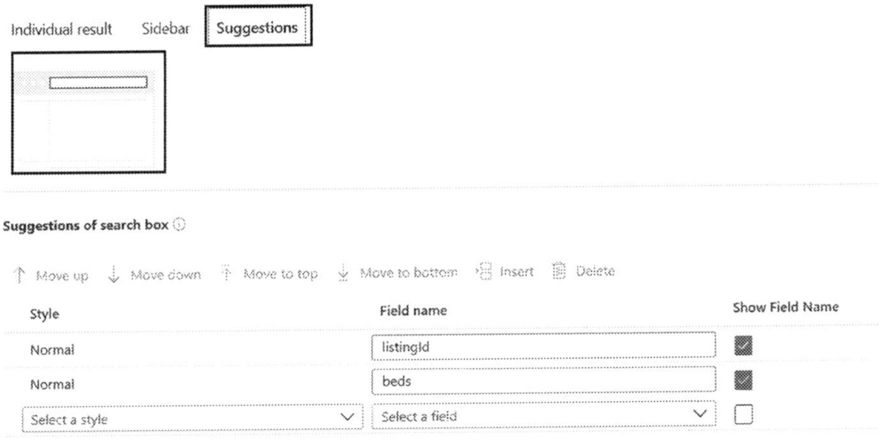

Style	Field name	Show Field Name
Normal	listingId	☑
Normal	beds	☑
Select a style	Select a field	☐

Figure 1-40. *Suggestions of search box*

Figures 1-38, 1-39, and 1-40 are shown with values I selected for the app.

Once this process is complete click Create Search App to generate the app page. It will ask you to download the HTML page. This page, named AzSearch is a plain HTML page with a few lines of smart code (Figure 1-41).

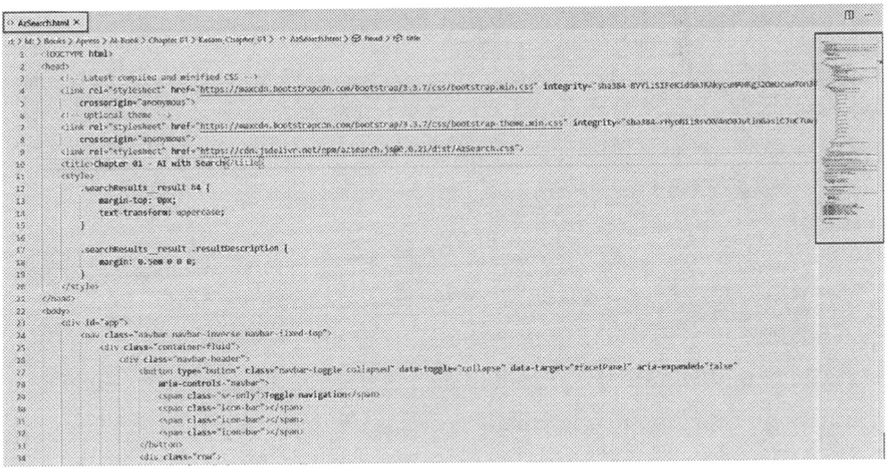

Figure 1-41. *Code view of* `AzSearch.html`

You can directly open this HTML file and run it on a browser (with Internet on), or you can push the file to the cloud, to have the app accessible with a public URL. Alternatively, you can use the code in your existing application.

I have used the cool feature of hosting a static website on Azure, offered by Microsoft Azure Storage, and uploaded the file. The results are shown in Figure 1-42.

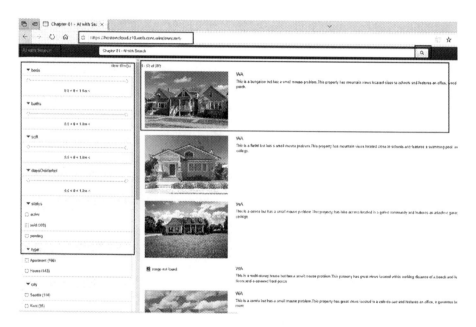

Figure 1-42.   *Search app on the cloud*

So, without writing a single line of code, just by importing the unstructured data to the Cognitive Search service, and enriching it with powerful cognitive skills, we created a smart, complex search application in almost no time, including all advanced search features.

To experience the real power of this service, Microsoft has created a web app named The JFK Files (Figure 1-43), using a huge unstructured data set in the form of images, documents, and so on. You can visit the app at https://jfkfiles2.azurewebsites.net/.

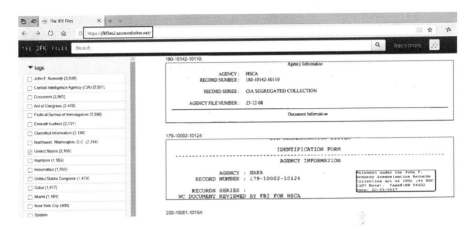

Figure 1-43.   *The JFK Files web app developed using Azure Cognitive Search*

Going through that site will help you appreciate using this service for your data. The exercise we just did, too, will definitely ease your journey as you get started.

Summary

This first chapter covered Azure Cognitive Search, how to create the service, and how you can leverage the power of Azure Cognitive Services to transform unstructured data into a manageable and searchable data set. I also presented the creation of a smart search application with writing almost no lines of code. Hopefully you have learned something new from the chapter. I recommend that you repeat the exercise as detailed, and get your hands dirty with the service. In the next chapter, I will walk you through the power Azure AI offers for back-end services.

CHAPTER 2

AI and Back-End Service Offerings

In Chapter 1, I introduced you to Azure Cognitive Search and explained how you can leverage the power of Azure AI with Search on the cloud, accomplishing multiple business objectives with ease. In this chapter, I introduce the cool AI capabilities offered by Microsoft Azure for your application back-end database service, Azure SQL. I will also describe the smart feature details, and show you how to enable this AI feature with a proper business workflow using Azure Automation.

Introduction to Azure SQL Database

As defined by Microsoft, "Azure SQL Database is the intelligent, scalable, relational database service built for the cloud. It is evergreen and always up to date, with AI-powered and automated features that optimize performance and durability for you." Azure SQL is a Database-as-a-Service offering from Microsoft Azure, which can be used to practice a relational SQL database on the cloud, eliminating any software or hardware installation tasks. The Compute and Storage options underlying the service leave you free to focus more on application development without being concerned with any on-demand database resource scaling.

This intelligent back-end service presents you with multiple advanced features, including the following.

- Automated backups

- Business continuity

- Easy migration

- Georeplication

- High availability

- Resource scaling

There are many others as well, but in this chapter, I focus on two smart areas:

- Intelligent Insights

- Automatic tuning

You can read more about this back-end offering by visiting `https://docs.microsoft.com/en-in/azure/azure-sql/`.

Intelligent Insights

Intelligent Insights is a unique capability of Azure built-in intelligence. It is used as a performance assessment for both Azure SQL Database and Azure SQL Managed Instance. Leveraging the built-in intelligent capabilities, Intelligent Insights monitors any event impeding database performance. With the help of AI, this service keeps monitoring database usage to detect any disruptive events that cause poor database performance.

Determination of these disruptive events is based on time taken and errors encountered with the query execution. Along with detecting such events, it also presents a clear analysis referred to as intelligent assessment of the issues. This analysis includes detailed root cause analysis (RCA) for database performance degradation along with recommendations for performance improvement, wherever possible.

At the time of writing, Intelligent Insights is in preview, and hence I do not provide further details on this subject.

Figure 2-1 presents a wider graphic view on how Intelligent Insights works.

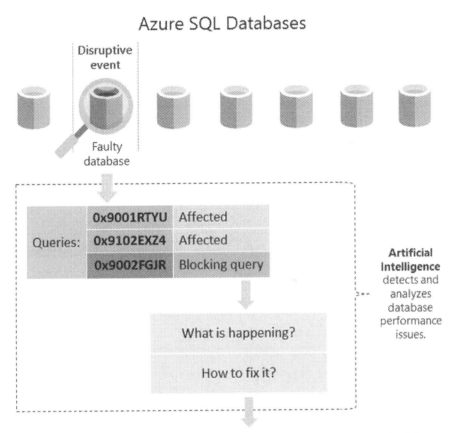

Figure 2-1. *Graphic depiction of how Intelligent Insights works (Image from https://docs.microsoft.com/en-us/azure/azure-sql/database/intelligent-insights-overview)*

Intelligent Insights provides following added value.

- Proactively monitoring the database using AI.

- Presents with required performance insights.

- Early detection of any events causing poor database performance.

- Presents with RCA of issues, if detected.

- Recommendations with respect to performance improvement.

- Capability to scale out with thousands of databases.

- Constructive impact on the total cost of ownership.

You can keep track of new updates coming for Intelligent Insights, along with exploring in how it works, by visiting https://docs.microsoft.com/en-us/azure/azure-sql/database/intelligent-insights-overview.

Note   At the time of writing, Intelligent Insights is in preview.

Automatic Tuning

Now let's dive into another smart service, automatic tuning, that comes with both Azure SQL Database and Azure SQL Managed Instance.

Note   In this chapter I cover exercises with Azure SQL Database. If you want to learn more about Azure SQL Managed Instance, you can visit https://docs.microsoft.com/en-us/azure/azure-sql/managed-instance/sql-managed-instance-paas-overview.

Azure SQL Database automatic tuning provides top performance and steady workloads through continuous performance tuning based on AI and machine learning. It is a fully managed intelligent service that continuously monitors the queries executed on an Azure SQL database, and automatically improves query performance. Unlike Intelligent Insights, this service focuses more on the query execution performance of the database. This performance tuning is achieved based on learning horizontally from all databases on Azure through AI and then dynamically improving the required tuning actions. Performance tuning is directly proportional to the period tuning is used on the database. This means you can expect the better performance tuning if you have the auto tuning option on for a longer period of time.

The following are some of the key features that make this service the one most recommended for Azure SQL workloads.

- *Safe:* Tuning operations performed on a database are completely safe with respect to performance of the intense workloads. Design considerations take care to not interfere with user workloads.

- *Smart timing:* Recommendations pulled from auto tuning are applied during the time when there is the lowest usage.

- *Workloads are priority:* To protect workload performance, the system sometimes disables auto tuning operations. It always favors workloads with top resource priority.

Working with Automatic Tuning

The auto tuning mechanism works based on ample successful learning achieved on millions of databases running on Microsoft Azure. When the service is enabled for an Azure SQL database instance, it continuously monitors the query execution taking place in the database and keeps seeking optimization opportunities. As mentioned earlier, these discoveries are based on horizontal learning. Once it finds and applies the tuning operations, it doesn't end there. It ensures positive performance improvement, after performing the tuning operation. Any regressed performance recommendations are proactively detected, and reverted on time. All the tuning operations are also recorded, presenting clear evidence of any improvement made to database resources.

Figure 2-2 graphically depicts the process of the auto tuning mechanism.

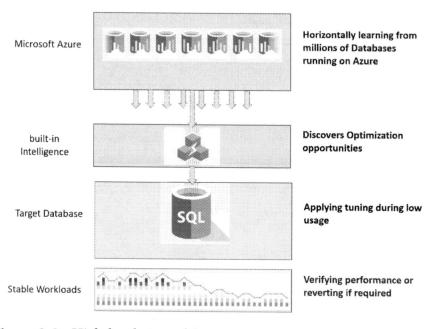

Figure 2-2. *High-level view of the auto tuning mechanism*

Note Azure SQL Database automatic tuning shares its core logic with the SQL Server automatic tuning feature in the database engine. For additional technical information on the built-in intelligence mechanism, see the documentation on SQL Server automatic tuning at `https://docs.microsoft.com/en-us/sql/relational-databases/automatic-tuning/automatic-tuning?view=sql-server-ver15`.

Automatic Tuning Options

At the time of writing, automatic tuning comes with three options, listed in Table 2-1, as recommendations to improve database performance.

Table 2-1. *Automatic Tuning Options*

Create Index	It identifies and create indexes that may help in performance optimization. After performing the operations, it also validates the improvements.
Drop Index	It identifies any duplicate indexes, or unused indexes from a suggested threshold period. Premium and Business Critical tiers do not support this option.
Force Last Good Plan	Identifies the good execution plans for queries and autocorrects the same. At the time of writing, this is the only option that applies on both Azure SQL Database and Azure SQL Managed Instance.

These options can be enabled manually via Azure Portal or can be configured to perform automatically. It depends on business requirements, technical requirements, and the design of the database you are working on. Again, you can enable this feature independently at the database level or directly at the server level, which will propagate the same settings to all the databases on that server. Enabling the method at the server level is recommended, as it provides seamless management and good control of databases if the database count is huge.

When you enable settings at the server level, the server uses the default automatic tuning settings, the Azure defaults, on all the databases under the server. As per the latest update in March 2020, the Azure defaults will be as follows.

- FORCE_LAST_GOOD_PLAN = enabled.

- CREATE_INDEX = disabled (earlier this was enabled).

- DROP_INDEX = disabled.

Enabling Automatic Tuning

There are three ways by which we can enable automatic tuning, both at the server level and the database level.

- Azure Portal

- REST API calls

- T-SQL commands

In this chapter I cover how you can enable automatic tuning using Azure Portal. You can explore the other two options on your own, as it all depends on your requirements and process approach.

Obviously, this all requires a valid Azure subscription. Enabling this feature, however, requires minimum permissions for the user. The following roles, listed in ascending order, will work.

- SQL Database Contributor

- SQL Server Contributor

- Contributor

- Owner

Enabling on Azure SQL Server

Once you have a valid subscription and the required role, open Azure
Portal. Navigate to your resource group; in this case it is AzureAI. Click
+Add => Type SQL Database or click SQL Database as shown in Figure 2-3.

This will present you with a window to enter details related to Azure
SQL Database.

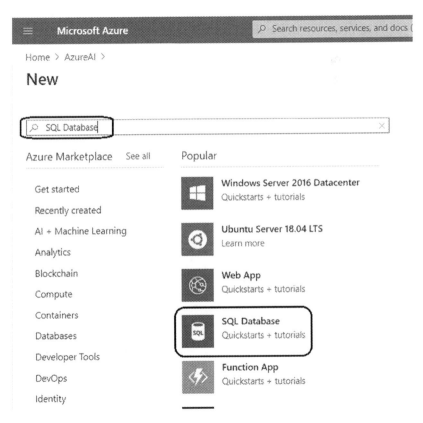

Figure 2-3. *Marketplace view to select the Azure resources to be*
created

Creating Azure SQL Server Database

You can select any existing server from the Server drop-down list or create a new one. Click Create New, as shown in Figure 2-4.

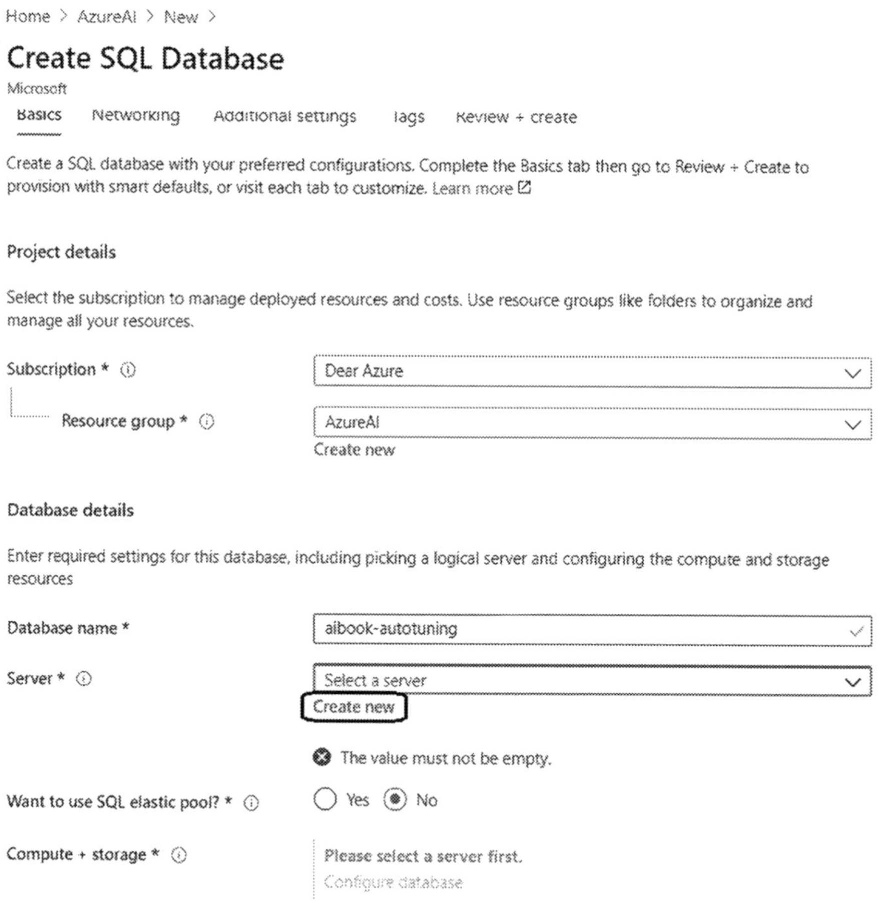

Home > AzureAI > New >

Create SQL Database
Microsoft

Basics   Networking   Additional settings   Tags   Review + create

Create a SQL database with your preferred configurations. Complete the Basics tab then go to Review + Create to provision with smart defaults, or visit each tab to customize. Learn more 🗗

Project details

Select the subscription to manage deployed resources and costs. Use resource groups like folders to organize and manage all your resources.

Subscription * ⓘ | Dear Azure   ⌄ |

    Resource group * ⓘ | AzureAI   ⌄ |
                            Create new

Database details

Enter required settings for this database, including picking a logical server and configuring the compute and storage resources

Database name * | aibook-autotuning   ✓ |

Server * ⓘ | Select a server   ⌄ |
                        Create new

                      ❌ The value must not be empty.

Want to use SQL elastic pool? * ⓘ   ◯ Yes ◉ No

Compute + storage * ⓘ | Please select a server first.
                                      Configure database

Figure 2-4. *Creating an Azure SQL database*

When you click on Create New, it will present you with another window, where you can provide the following mandatory details related to Azure SQL Server.

- *Server Name:* Name of the server of your choice. The name will appear as `<Name>.database.windows.net`.

- *Server Admin Login:* This is the Admin username to be used for login purposes

- *Password and Confirm Password:* This field will contain the password for the given Admin login username.

- *Location:* This is the location to which this resource will be deployed.

Once you have entered all the required details, click OK to proceed, as seen in Figure 2-5.

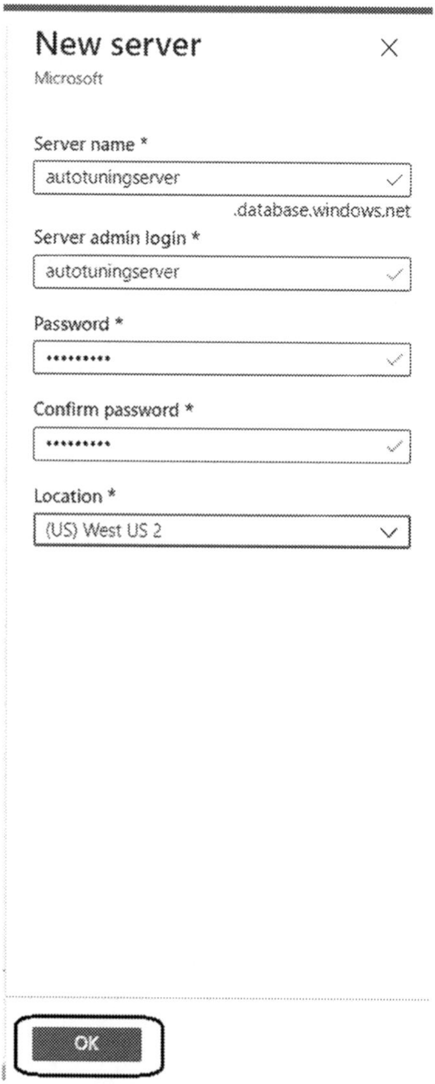

New server   ×

Microsoft

Server name *

autotuningserver

.database.windows.net

Server admin login *

autotuningserver

Password *

••••••••

Confirm password *

••••••••

Location *

(US) West US 2

OK

Figure 2-5. *Creating the SQL server*

For this exercise, we will use the default values for all sections required to create the resource.

After you have entered the details, last is the Review + Create tab. Click Create to proceed with the validation and deployment process, as shown in Figure 2-6.

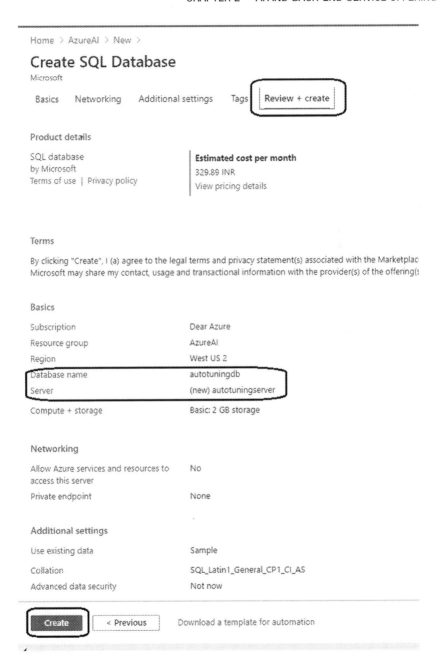

Home > AzureAI > New >

Create SQL Database
Microsoft

Basics   Networking   Additional settings   Tags   Review + create

Product details

SQL database
by Microsoft
Terms of use | Privacy policy

Estimated cost per month
329.89 INR
View pricing details

Terms

By clicking "Create", I (a) agree to the legal terms and privacy statement(s) associated with the Marketplac
Microsoft may share my contact, usage and transactional information with the provider(s) of the offering(s

Basics

Subscription	Dear Azure
Resource group	AzureAI
Region	West US 2
Database name	autotuningdb
Server	(new) autotuningserver
Compute + storage	Basic: 2 GB storage

Networking

Allow Azure services and resources to access this server	No
Private endpoint	None

Additional settings

Use existing data	Sample
Collation	SQL_Latin1_General_CP1_CI_AS
Advanced data security	Not now

Create   < Previous   Download a template for automation

Figure 2-6. *Review + Create tab for the Azure SQL server creation*

Once the resource is created, open the resource group to see the newly created Azure SQL server and Azure SQL database listed under resources. You can navigate to a resource via many paths, using the resource group setting is the best. Select the Azure SQL server as shown in Figure 2-7.

Figure 2-7. *Newly created resources listed under a resource group*

There are two ways you can navigate to the page to enable tuning on the Azure SQL Server resource page.

- Overview ➤ Features ➤ Performance ➤ Azure Tuning Box.

- Under Intelligent Performance, select Automatic Tuning.

Both of these options are highlighted in Figure 2-8.

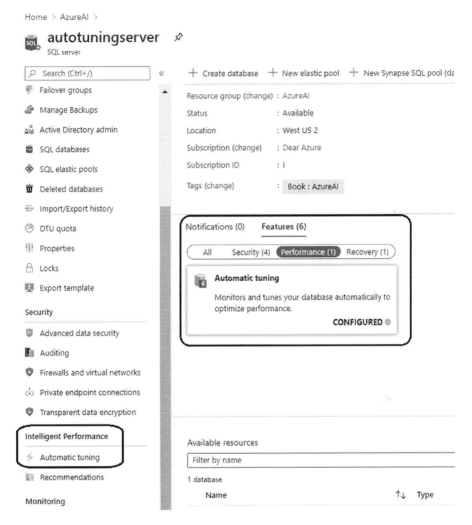

Figure 2-8. *Options to open the page for enabling automatic tuning*

Both of these options will lead to same page, shown in Figure 2-9.

Figure 2-9. *Page to enable automatic tuning at the server level*

In Figure 2-9 you will notice by default the Inherit option is set when Azure Defaults are on. Also, Azure Defaults as per the latest updates are in place.

Now you can change the options as required and configure databases not to inherit the options set for this server.

So, with few clicks you were able to apply the AI and machine learning back-end feature for your Azure SQL server.

Enabling on Azure SQL Database

Open the new database you created in the preceding steps. Azure SQL Database follows the same navigation path to open up the automatic tuning options enabling page, as displayed in Figure 2-10.

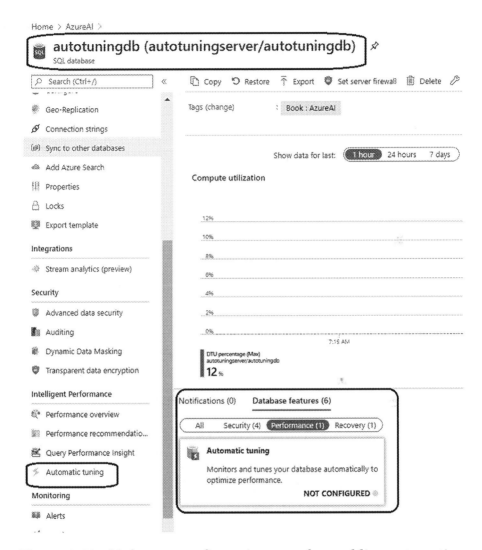

Figure 2-10. *Links to to configuration page for enabling automatic tuning*

Clicking either of the highlighted options shown in Figure 2-10, will open the page to enable automatic tuning, this time with a few different options, as shown in Figure 2-11.

Figure 2-11. *Page to enable automatic tuning at the database level*

Here it will present you with an option to inherit from the SQL server. At any time, you can select Don't Inherit and change the tuning options as per your project requirements.

For this example, let's select Don't Inherit and set DROP INDEX too Off. Once done, click Apply to enable the change.

You will notice that once you change the option from Server, Azure Portal will present you with a warning, indicating that inheritance is the recommended approach (Figure 2-12). For this exercise, I will make the change and click Apply.

Figure 2-12. *Page to enable automatic tuning at the database level with a warning message*

Here I am just trying to show you how easy it is to enable the feature and make the best use of the AI capabilities for your back-end services.

Viewing Automatic Tuning Recommendations

I have shown you how the automatic tuning works and how you can enable it in your Azure SQL Database. In this exercise we will learn how you can view the automatic tuning recommendations.

Familiarity with the intelligent recommendations provided by the automatic tuning service will help the application team consider these factors in future database designing. In addition, it can help us understand the execution behavior of workloads taking place in the database and to make changes appropriately.

These recommendations can be viewed in Azure Management Portal and can be retrieved in three ways:

- REST APIs

- T-SQL

- PowerShell commands

Here I will demonstrate the ethod using PowerShell commands.

As a part of this exercise, we create the following resources:

- Azure Automation account

- Logic Apps

Runbook with a PowerShell script in Automation account will retrieve the automatic tuning recommendations for the database provided. They can then be viewed in Azure Portal. Further, the Logic Apps workflow will get these recommendations from the runbook, and send them as mail notifications to any configured user.

Note   You can also use Power Automate in place of Logic Apps.

Azure Automation Account

I will create an Azure Automation account, and have a runbook created with PowerShell scripts. This script will retrieve the automatic tuning recommendations and present them in Azure Portal.

1. Open Azure Portal, and search for Automations Account.

2. Create a new Automation account or select an existing account.

3. Under Automation Account, create a new runbook with the details shown in Figure 2-13, and then click Create.

Figure 2-13. *Creating a runbook*

    4.   Copy the following PowerShell script:

```
#Login-AzAccount
$subscriptions = ("Your Subscription")
$rgs = ("Resource group name")
# Get credentials
```

```
$Conn = Get-AutomationConnection -Name AzureRunAsConnection
Connect-AzAccount -ServicePrincipal -Tenant $Conn.TenantID
-ApplicationId $Conn.ApplicationID -CertificateThumbprint
$Conn.CertificateThumbprint
# Define the resource types
$resourceTypes = ("Microsoft.Sql/servers/databases")
$advisors = ("CreateIndex", "DropIndex");
$results = @()
# Loop through all subscriptions
foreach($subscriptionId in $subscriptions) {
    Select-AzSubscription -SubscriptionId $subscriptionId |
    Out-Null
    # Loop through all resource groups
    foreach($rg in $rgs) {
        #$rgname = $rg.ResourceGroupName;
         $rgname = $rg
        # Loop through all resource types
        foreach($resourceType in $resourceTypes) {
            $resources = Get-AzResource -ResourceGroupName
            $rgname -ResourceType $resourceType
            # Loop through all databases
            # Extract resource groups, servers, and databases
            foreach ($resource in $resources) {
                $resourceId = $resource.ResourceId
                if ($resourceId -match ".*RESOURCEGROUPS/
                (?<content>.*)/PROVIDERS.*") {
                    $ResourceGroupName = $matches['content']
                } else {
                    continue
                }
```

```
if ($resourceId -match ".*SERVERS/
(?<content>.*)/DATABASES.*") {
    $ServerName = $matches['content']
} else {
    continue
}
if ($resourceId -match ".*/DATABASES/
(?<content>.*)") {
    $DatabaseName = $matches['content']
} else {
    continue
}
# Skip if master
if ($DatabaseName -eq "master") {
    continue
}
# Loop through all automatic tuning
recommendation types
foreach ($advisor in $advisors) {
    $recs = Get-AzSqlDatabaseRecommendedAction
    -ResourceGroupName $ResourceGroupName
    -ServerName $ServerName   -DatabaseName
    $DatabaseName -AdvisorName $advisor
    foreach ($r in $recs) {
        if ($r.State.CurrentValue -eq "Active") {
            $object = New-Object -TypeName
            PSObject
            $object | Add-Member -Name
            'SubscriptionId' -MemberType
            Noteproperty -Value $subscriptionId
```

```
                          $object | Add-Member
                          -Name 'ResourceGroupName'
                          -MemberType Noteproperty -Value
                          $r.ResourceGroupName
                          $object | Add-Member -Name
                          'ServerName' -MemberType
                          Noteproperty -Value $r.ServerName
                          $object | Add-Member -Name
                          'DatabaseName' -MemberType
                          Noteproperty -Value $r.DatabaseName
                          $object | Add-Member -Name 'Script'
                          -MemberType Noteproperty -Value
                          $r.ImplementationDetails.Script
                          $results += $object
                        }
                      }
                  }
                }
            }
        }
}

# Format and output results for the email
$table = $results | Format-List
Write-Output $table
```

   5.   Now paste that PowerShell script in the code pane
        and click Save. It will look like Figure 2-14.

Figure 2-14. *PowerShell script to retrieve automatic tuning recommendations*

Note   You need to provide your subscription and the resource group name that your database resides in. Also, if you encounter any error in running this script, make sure you have imported all the required PowerShell modules to your Automation account. You can learn more at `https://docs.microsoft.com/en-us/azure/automation/automation-runbook-gallery`.

---

6.   Click Publish ➤ Start to see the recommendations
     in the Output window, if there are any, as displayed
     in Figure 2-15. You will not necessarily always have
     recommendations.

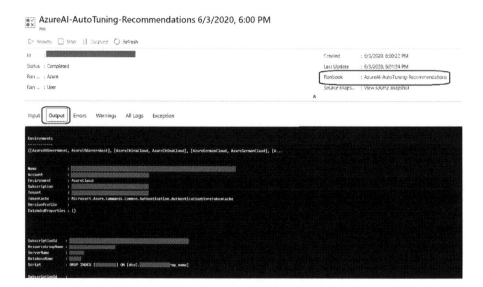

Figure 2-15. *Output after publishing the PowerShell scripts and
running the runbook*

Sent Email Notification with Recommendations

You can schedule this runbook to run every day, week, month, or for
any custom period. If your business requirements dictatew that these
recommendations need to be retrieved once a month and sent to an
application architect or concerned team member, you can go through the
same process and make changes accordingly.

In this scenario we have two options, Power Automate workflow and
Azure Logic Apps orkflow. Both come with the required connectors for
Azure Automation.

For this instance I will use Azure Logic Apps, so let's get started.

1. Open Azure Portal ➤ Search for Logic Apps ➤ Create a new Logic App.

2. Open the LogicApp designer and select Start With Blank Template.

3. Now as we need to have this recommendation once a month, we need to have a schedule trigger in place.

    Search for the name Schedule and select the trigger Recurrence. This will help you to schedule the workflow to trigger according to the requirement. The example shown in Figure 2-16 has it configured to run once a month with the initial time zone and start time set.

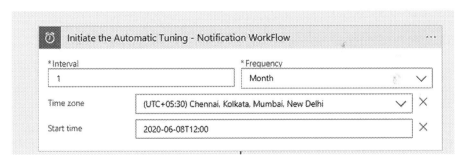

Figure 2-16. *Azure Logic Apps trigger connector for scheduling the workflow*

4. Next search for the connector Azure Automation and then select the action name, Create Job. Add the required details of the Azure Automation account and runbook created, as displayed in Figure 2-17.

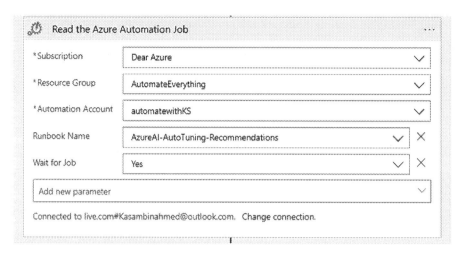

Figure 2-17. *Azure Logic Apps action connector for running automation job*

This connector will have the selected runbook to execute. Next we need to read the output content from the preceding connector.

5. Again, search for the connector Azure Automation and select the action name Get Job output.

    For Job ID, enter the ID from preceding step, as seen in Figure 2-18.

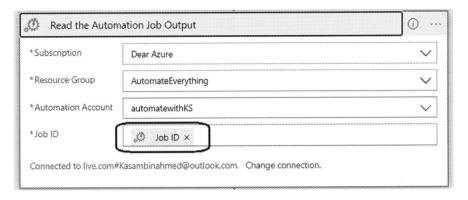

Figure 2-18. Azure Logic Apps action connector for reading the automation job output

6. Next, we need to send a notification via email with the job output, the automatic tuning recommendations. Select the connector Outlook.com and then select the action Send Mail. Finally, your workflow will look like Figure 2-19.

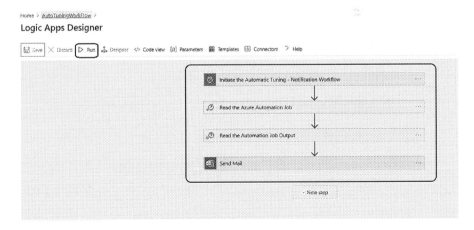

Figure 2-19. An overview of the Azure Logic App workflow

Note   For these Azure Automation connectors, ensure you authenticate using the same credentials, with a valid Azure subscription and the required Azure Automation account.

When you click Run to trigger the flow manually, wait for few seconds for the email to arrive at the configured email ID. Figure 2-20 shows the notification that the message was sent and you have accomplished your business objective.

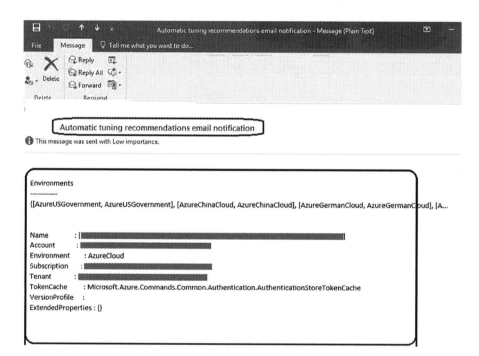

Figure 2-20. *Notification received in inbox via Azure Logic App flow*

Summary

This chapter introduced the built-in AI capabilities presented by Azure SQL Database, a back-end Database-as-a-Service offered by Microsoft Azure. We also explored how it works and adds value in your applications. You also learned how to enable this smart feature at both the database and server level. Finally, we looked at how you can share the intelligent recommendations as email notifications using Azure Automation and the Azure Logic Apps service. You should further explore these features for your workloads to determine what provides the best performance output. I also suggest that you read Microsoft the documentation, as it is an excellent source of information. In the next chapter, we turn to AI offerings with Azure Integration Services.

CHAPTER 3

Working with Azure iPaaS

Chapter 2 covered built-in AI capabilities with back-end services and explained how you can enable and leverage the power of these built-in capabilities with Azure SQL, accomplishing smart monitoring and performance objectives with ease. This chapter details the grand AI capabilities offered by Microsoft Azure with Integration Platform as a Service (iPaaS). Now, before you can understand what iPaaS is, you must understand what integration is and how it is used in any organization.

What Is Integration?

For any big or small organization, there are various systems and components that are at play. On one side of the spectrum, we have the customer, third-party agreements that organizations have for data exchange, the intelligent assistants that provide value and support to customers, and the classic web and mobile apps. These primarily front-end components require heavy user interaction. On the other side of the spectrum, we have systems that facilitate machine learning and AI systems that analyze the huge amounts of data, the third-party Software-as-a-Service (SaaS) services that are used in organization (e.g., SAP, ERP systems like Salesforce, etc), any containerized or in-house apps developed by the organization, and the data that are generated.

© Kasam Shaikh 2020
K. Shaikh, *Demystifying Azure AI*, https://doi.org/10.1007/978-1-4842-6219-1_3

In such a complex ecosystem, none of the applications can work in silos; these systems need to communicate with each other. Through this unification, the organization can provide value to its stakeholders. Integration Services provides the ability to unify the disparate systems, make them function as one, and deliver maximum value.

Expectations from an Integration Platform

Based on the need for integration in a complex ecosystem, several things are expected from modern-day integration platforms.

- Ability to securely expose APIs to external and internal systems.

- Ability to orchestrate processes and automate tasks.

- Secure and reliable messaging system to enable cross-systems communications.

- Ability to support reactive style of programming via use of events.

- Easy to develop.

- Less onboarding time for developers.

- Codeless as much as possible.

- Should support old integration patterns as well as modern ones.

What Is iPaaS?

In simple terms, when a cloud provides a integration platform as a part of its cloud offering, it is generally termed an iPaaS. Such a platform allows organizations to develop workflows and integrations that can be purely cloud-based or hybrid in nature by connecting to the on-premises systems.

Gartner defines iPaaS as "a suite of cloud services enabling development, execution, and governance of integration flows connecting any combination of on premises and cloud-based processes, services, applications and data within individual or across multiple organizations" (see `https://www.gartner.com/en/information-technology/glossary/information-platform-as-a-service-ipaas`).

Azure Integration Services

To meet the expectations for an integration platform, Microsoft has come up with a suite of services that, when used together, allow us to create complex integrations that are easy to develop. These services allow us to achieve various integrations, ranging from standard application integration to business-to-business (B2B) integration.

At the time of writing, the Azure Integration Services suite consists of the following services.

- *Azure API Management:* This service securely exposes the APIs for external and internal use.

- *Azure Logic Apps:* This service provides an intuitive and easy way to create integration workflows.

- *Azure Service Bus:* This service provides enterprise-grade reliable messaging.

- *Azure Event Grid:* This service provides the ability to develop reactive systems based on events.

Let's take a brief look at each of these services.

Azure API Management

Azure APIs, denoted by the icon in Figure 3-1, serve as a secure way of managing APIs.

Figure 3-1. *Azure API Management icon*

- Azure API Management allows us to securely expose the integrations that we develop. It allows us to expose HTTP-based web APIs that we can create using Azure Logic Apps, functions, or even custom web APIs using the Azure App Service.

- Because it can mask the back-end URLs, we can create URLs that are more discoverable and marketable.

- Azure API Management supports product- and subscription-based access to the APIs so that only intended users can use the APIs.

- Azure API Management has a powerful policy engine that allows us to implement various restrictions like IP filtering, allowing CORS calls, limiting the rate of calls for the API, implementing OAUTH 2.0 and OpenID authorization for the APIs, and so on.

- Azure API Management sports a highly customizable open source developer portal that can be used to let consumers of the API try out the APIs.

Azure Logic Apps

Azure Logic Apps, denoted by the icon shown in Figure 3-2, reside at the heart of the iPaaS story of Microsoft.

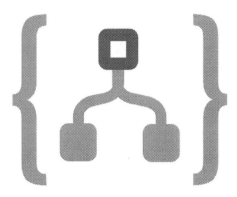

Figure 3-2. *Azure Logic Apps icon*

- Logic Apps are completely serverless as they Logic Apps runtime engine is completely abstracted from developers and maintained by Microsoft internally. This makes Logic Apps a true Platform-as-a-Service (PaaS) offering.

- Logic Apps allows us to automate workflows and orchestrate business processes. These integrations can range from simple data management to enterprise, B2B, and app integrations.

- Logic Apps works with a designer-first approach, where the development is done using a easy-to-use designer (quite similar to the orchestration designer of BizTalk).

- The Logic Apps platform has more than 300 connectors that help to develop lightweight integration.

- Logic Apps are templatized and provide out-of-the-box templates for common integration scenarios.

- These features serve to let developers who are not familiar with enterprise integration churn out workflows quickly.

- Features like Integration Account, inline code, expressions, on-premises data gateway, and custom connectors let hard-core integration developers develop mission-critical orchestrations.

- Azure Logic Apps can be run completely on the cloud or inside your virtual network using the Integrated Service Environment.

Azure Functions

The following are some things you should know about Azure Functions, denoted by the icon in Figure 3-3, the serverless offering from Microsoft.

Figure 3-3. *Azure Functions icon*

- Azure Functions is not part of the Azure Integration Services suite, but it is equally important, as Azure Functions is used as a utility function to provide functionality that Logic Apps cannot provide.

- Azure Functions presents another side of the story of running serverless workloads. Azure functions are just small pieces of code that run on the Azure Functions runtime platform.

- They have plethora of bindings and triggers. Examples of bindings would be the Azure Blob storage binding, Queue bindings, and Send Grid bindings. Triggers include the Event Grid trigger, HTTP, webhook, and timer triggers.

- Azure Functions is suitable for people from a development background, as it offers the freedom to author code according to the need. This gives developers the ability to develop and debug functions locally before deploying them to Azure.

- Azure Functions is multilingual and supports several development languages, from C#, JavaScript, and PowerShell to F#.

- Azure Functions can be deployed to either a fixed-costs Azure App Service plan, or they can be deployed to a consumption-based plan, making them serverless in nature. Azure Functions can also be deployed as containerized docker apps.

Azure Service Bus

Here are some important points about Azure Service Bus, denoted by the icon shown in Figure 3-4.

Figure 3-4. *Azure Service Bus icon*

- Azure Service Bus is a fully managed cloud messaging service for enterprise-level messaging.

- An enterprise messaging system is supposed to be highly secure, reliable, and scalable. Azure Service Bus is highly secure, as the data traveling through the service bus are encrypted during transit. It is highly reliable because it provides guaranteed delivery of the messages within its designated time. It also provides the ability to move messages to dead letter queues to process orphaned messages.

- Azure Service Bus comes with different plans, including Basic, Standard, and Premium, which are suitable for different production loads. This makes Azure Service

Bus highly scalable, as we can change the plans according to our needs.

- Azure Service Bus supports the publish subscribe mechanism, which is used extensively while creating asynchronous integrations.

- Azure Service Bus supports the classic first in, first out configuration, which is used in integrations where order of reception of messages is very important.

- Azure Service Bus supports one-subscriber linear communication between systems using Queues and fanned-out communication using Topics, which allow multiple subscribers to read the same message.

- Azure Service Bus allows developers to establish secure integrations between on-premises systems and cloud systems, thus enabling hybrid integrations.

Azure Event Grid

The following are some important points about Azure Event Grid, which is denoted by the icon shown in Figure 3-5.

Figure 3-5. *Azure Event Grid icon*

- Azure Event Grid is a fully Microsoft managed routing service offering of Azure that delivers event notifications using a lightweight HTTP call. The Azure Event Grid is part of the Azure backbone, and by default, many Azure activities that we perform trigger an event. The simplest examples would be when a blob is created or deleted, when a resource is deleted, and so on. There are lot of events available for us to react to.

- This lightweight event notification allows us to develop event-driven solutions that work on the publish subscribe mechanism. This promotes a very loosely coupled style of solution architecture.

- A great feature of Event Grid is that it supports the publication of built-in Azure events as well as our own custom events (which can pe published to custom Event Grid Topics). Interested parties can then subscribe to these published events.

- Azure Event Grid provides the option of making filters available to subscribers so they can choose what they want to subscribe to.

- Azure Event Grid has a very high throughput and resiliency.

- It is very cheap, and the billing is done per event.

Now that we know what various services are offered in the Azure Integration Services suite, we can look at what integrations we can create using Azure Logic Apps and Azure Cognitive Services.

Modern-Day Intelligent Workflows

In today's world, AI is quickly gaining acceptance in various processes adopted by organizations. AI allows organizations to automate complex processes where human-like reasoning is required. Here are some examples.

- Analyzing the feedback provided by the consumers of a product marketed by an organization.

- Automating customer service issue creation based on the complaints submitted by consumers.

In such scenarios it is imperative that we have services that provide various human reasoning abilities, like face recognition, voice recognition, natural language processing and understanding, emotion detection, text analytics, and so on. Microsoft Azure provides various services to accomplish these tasks mentioned above. Because Azure Cognitive Services is provided to developers as web APIs, all of these can be used inside Logic Apps to create intelligent workflows.

Let us look at a particular use case where we can use Logic Apps and Azure Cognitive Services to create modern-day intelligent integration solutions.

Illegal Parking Management

Illegal parking management is an important functions for many local governments. Consider the following scenario.

- A local municipal body has provided various parking spaces across the city for two-wheeled vehicles.

- Drivers can park their vehicles in these designated parking spaces only.

- If two-wheeled vehicles are found outside of these areas, officers of the law fine the driver of the vehicle. They capture a photograph of the vehicle and issue a ticket for the infraction.

- When law officers capture photographs of the vehicle, the driver or other people sometimes get captured in the photograph.

- To avoid being sued by the people captured in the photos, it is necessary that the faces of the people in these photographs be blurred before the photographs are made public.

Figure 3-6 shows the workflow that we can use to achieve the blurring of the faces in the photographs captured by the law officers.

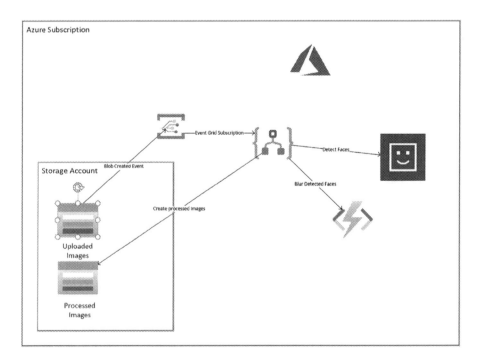

Figure 3-6. *High-level architecture workflow*

The workflow consists of the following steps.

1. The officers capture an image and the application on their mobile device uploads the image to an Azure Storage account as blobs.

2. The images are upload to a container called `uploads`. This triggers a `Microsoft.Storage.BlobCreated` event on Azure Event Grid.

3. A Logic App subscribes to the blob creation event when it happens on the `uploads` container.

4. The Logic App sends the URL of the blob created to the Face API (Azure Cognitive Service). The Face API detects the faces in the image and sends the coordinates of the all the detected images.

5. The Logic App sends the response from the Face API to an Azure function that blurs the faces in the images and returns the processed image as a base64 string.

6. The Logic App creates a new blob in the `processed-images` container and deletes the original blob from the `uploads` container.

Next let's look at how we can create this workflow in a step-by-step fashion.

Creating a Resource Group and Storage Account

We must create a resource group, a storage account, and containers in which to store and upload the images. Follow the step-by-step instructions given here to create the storage account and its containers.

1. Log on to Azure Portal (`https://portal.azure.com/`).

2. Click + Create A Resource, as shown in Figure 3-7.

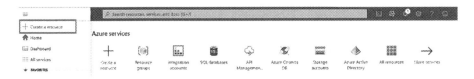

Figure 3-7. *Creating a resource in Azure Portal*

3. In the Search bar, enter Storage Account , as
    illustrated in Figure 3-8, and press Enter.

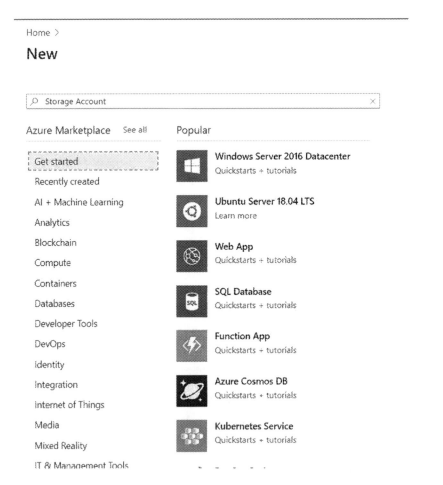

Figure 3-8. *Searching for a storage account in Azure Marketplace in
Azure Portal*

4.   Select the Storage Account as shown in Figure 3-9.

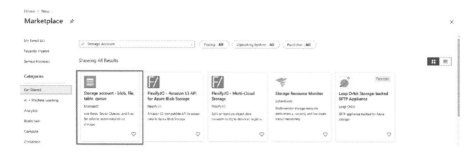

Figure 3-9. *Selecting a storage account*

5.   Click Create, as highlighted in Figure 3-10.

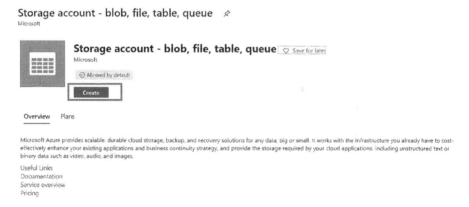

Figure 3-10. *Creating a storage account in Azure Portal*

6.   Select the proper subscription and click Create New to create a new resource group. Enter the name you will use for the resource group, as shown in Figure 3-11.

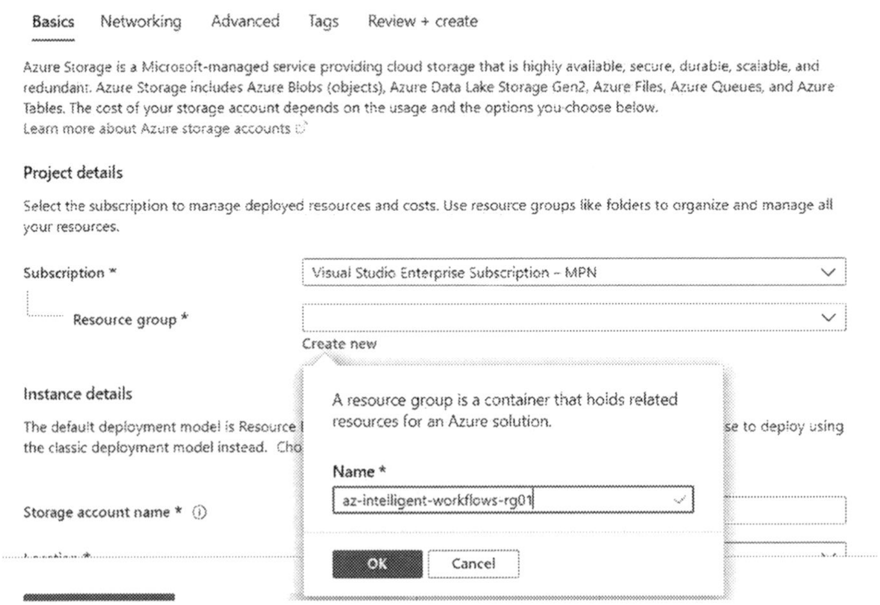

Basics   Networking   Advanced   Tags   Review + create

Azure Storage is a Microsoft-managed service providing cloud storage that is highly available, secure, durable, scalable, and redundant. Azure Storage includes Azure Blobs (objects), Azure Data Lake Storage Gen2, Azure Files, Azure Queues, and Azure Tables. The cost of your storage account depends on the usage and the options you choose below.
Learn more about Azure storage accounts ⏷

Project details

Select the subscription to manage deployed resources and costs. Use resource groups like folders to organize and manage all your resources.

Subscription *   Visual Studio Enterprise Subscription – MPN   ∨

        Resource group *   ∨
                          Create new

Instance details

The default deployment model is Resource | | se to deploy using
the classic deployment model instead.   Cho

Storage account name * ⓘ

A resource group is a container that holds related resources for an Azure solution.

Name *

az-intelligent-workflows-rg01   ∨

OK   Cancel

Figure 3-11. *Creating a new resource group*

> 7. Enter a unique name for the storage account and other settings as shown in Figure 3-12.

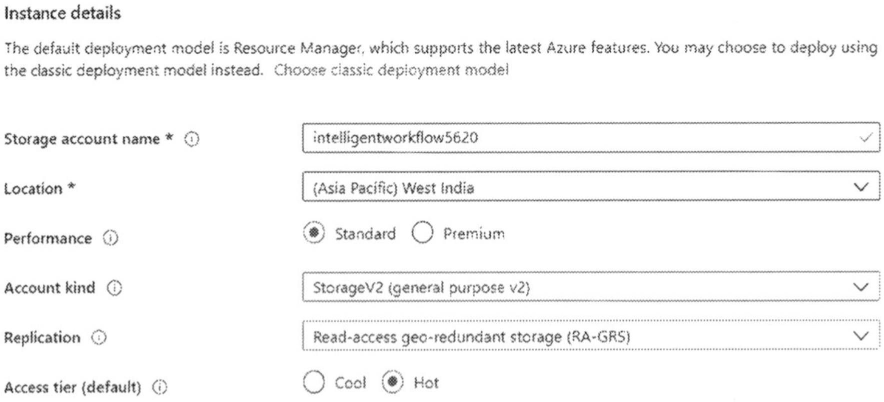

Instance details

The default deployment model is Resource Manager, which supports the latest Azure features. You may choose to deploy using the classic deployment model instead. Choose classic deployment model

Storage account name * ⓘ   intelligentworkflow5620   ∨

Location *   (Asia Pacific) West India   ∨

Performance ⓘ   ⦿ Standard ○ Premium

Account kind ⓘ   StorageV2 (general purpose v2)   ∨

Replication ⓘ   Read-access geo-redundant storage (RA-GRS)   ∨

Access tier (default) ⓘ   ○ Cool ⦿ Hot

Figure 3-12. *Details added for the new storage account*

8. We won't change other details in this exercise. Once
    you are done, click Review + Create. This launches a
    validation of the values provided in the form. Once
    the validations is complete, click Create to start
    deployment of the storage account.

9. Once the deployment is complete, the message
    shown in Figure 3-13 should be visible on the screen.

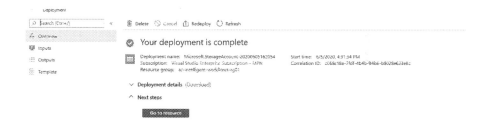

Figure 3-13. *Deployment completion message*

10. Click Go To Resource to navigate to the resource.

11. We will now add the containers to the storage
    account to store the uploaded and processed
    images. Click the Containers tab as shown in
    Figure 3-14.

Figure 3-14. *Link to open storage containers*

12. Click the Container button as shown in Figure 3-15.

Figure 3-15. *Add a new container*

13. Enter `upload` as the name of container and under Public Access, select Blob, as shown in Figure 3-16. Click Create to create the container.

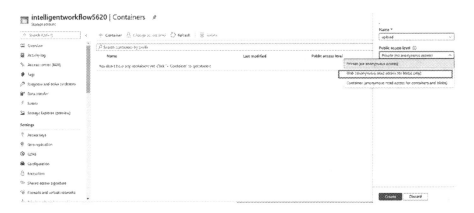

Figure 3-16. *Options to create a new storage container*

14. Similarly, create a container named `processed-images`.

This completes the process of creating the containers to upload the images.

Creating an Azure Function to Blur Faces

We will next create an Azure function to blur the faces in the images. To create an Azure function, the following components need to be installed on the development machine.

1. Visual Studio Code

2. .NET Core 3.1

3. Azure Functions Core Tools (see `https://docs.microsoft.com/en-us/azure/azure-functions/functions-run-local?tabs=windows%2Ccsharp%2Cbash` for installation instructions).

4. The Azure Functions extension installed for Visual Studio Code (`https://docs.microsoft.com/en-us/azure/azure-functions/functions-develop-vs-code?tabs=csharp`).

5. C# extension for Visual Studio Code (`https://code.visualstudio.com/docs/languages/csharp`).

We start by creating a project for Azure Functions.

1. Open the command prompt and run the commands shown in Figure 3-17.

```
Command Prompt

C:\>mkdir az-blur-faces-af01

C:\>cd az-blur-faces-af01

C:\az-blur-faces-af01>
```

Figure 3-17. *Commands for creating a project for Azure Functions*

2. We will now create the Azure Functions project
    inside this directory. Run the following command.

    func init -dotnet

    This will create an Azure Functions project with a
    dotnet runtime. Launch Visual Studio Code from
    this folder as shown in Figure 3-18.

```
C:\az-blur-faces-af01>func init --dotnet

Writing C:\az-blur-faces-af01\.vscode\extensions.json

C:\az-blur-faces-af01>code .
```

Figure 3-18. *Command to launch Visual Studio Code*

You should see files created that are shown in
Figure 3-19.

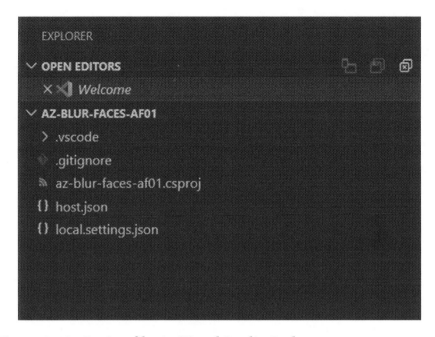

Figure 3-19. *Project files in Visual Studio Code*

3. Copy the following code inside the project.

az-blur-faces-af01.zip

You have now created an HTTP-triggered Azure function that we will call from the Logic App.

4. Deploy the Azure function to Azure Portal in the same resource group that we used to create the Azure storage account.

That completes the development of the Azure function.

Creating an Integration Account and Uploading the Transformation

To simplify the data that are fed to the Azure function we just created, we will combine some data from the Azure Event Grid and the response from the Face API. Hence, we need to create an Integration Account that will store our JSON to JSON transformation map. To learn more about Integration Account, see https://docs.microsoft.com/en-us/ azure/logic-apps/logic-apps-enterprise-integration-create-integration-account#:~:text=Before%20you%20can%20build%20 enterprise,with%20your%20logic%20app%20workflows.

Following these step-by-step instructions to create the Integration Account.

1. Log on to Azure Portal.

2. Click Create A Resource as shown in Figure 3-20.

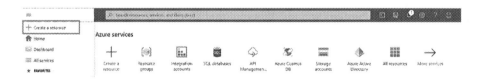

Figure 3-20. *Creating a new resource*

3. Navigate to Integration and click Integration Account as shown in Figure 3-21.

Figure 3-21. *Creating an Integration Account*

4. Fill out details in the form as shown in Figure 3-22 and then click Review + Create. Once the validation is complete, click Create.

Home > New >

Integration Account

Project details

Select the subscription to manage deployed resources and costs. Use resource groups like folders to organize and manage all your resources.

Subscription *	Visual Studio Enterprise Subscription – MPN ∨
Resource group *	az-intelligent-workflows-rg01 ∨
	Create new

Instance details

Integration account name *	az-intelligent-workflows-int-accnt01 ✓
Select the location	(•) Region ( ) Integration Service Environment
Location *	West India ∨
Pricing Tier *	Free ∨
Log Analytics ⓘ	(On **Off**)

| Review + create | < Previous : Basics | Next : Tags > | Download a template for automation ⓘ |

Figure 3-22. *Details for Integration Account*

5. The deployment for Integration Account will take few minutes. Once the deployment is finished, we can start using Integration Account.

6. Navigate to Integration Account. Click Maps as shown in Figure 3-23.

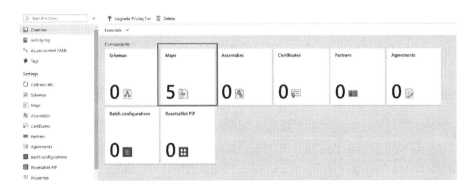

Figure 3-23. *Selecting the Maps option*

7. Click Add.

8. Fill out the details as shown in Figure 3-24 and upload the file indicated in the Map field. Click OK.

Figure 3-24. *Adding Map details*

This completes the process to upload the mapping file to Integration Account.

Next, let's create a Face API subscription in our account.

Creating a Face API Subscription

We need to create a subscription to Face API, which is a part of Azure Cognitive Services.

1. Log on to Azure Portal.

2. Click Create A Resource as shown in Figure 3-25.

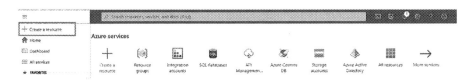

Figure 3-25.   *Creating a new resource*

3. Select AI + Machine Learning and then click Face, as shown in Figure 3-26.

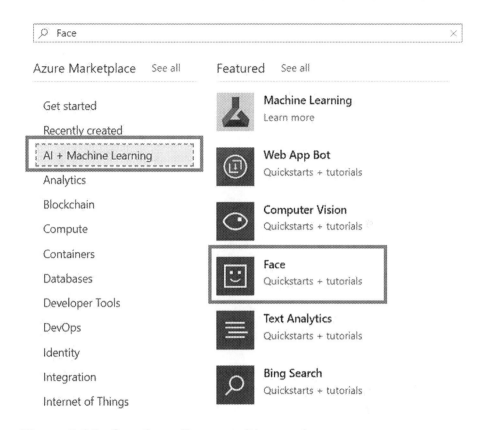

Figure 3-26. *Creating a Face cognitive service*

4. Populate the form as shown in Figure 3-27 and click Create.

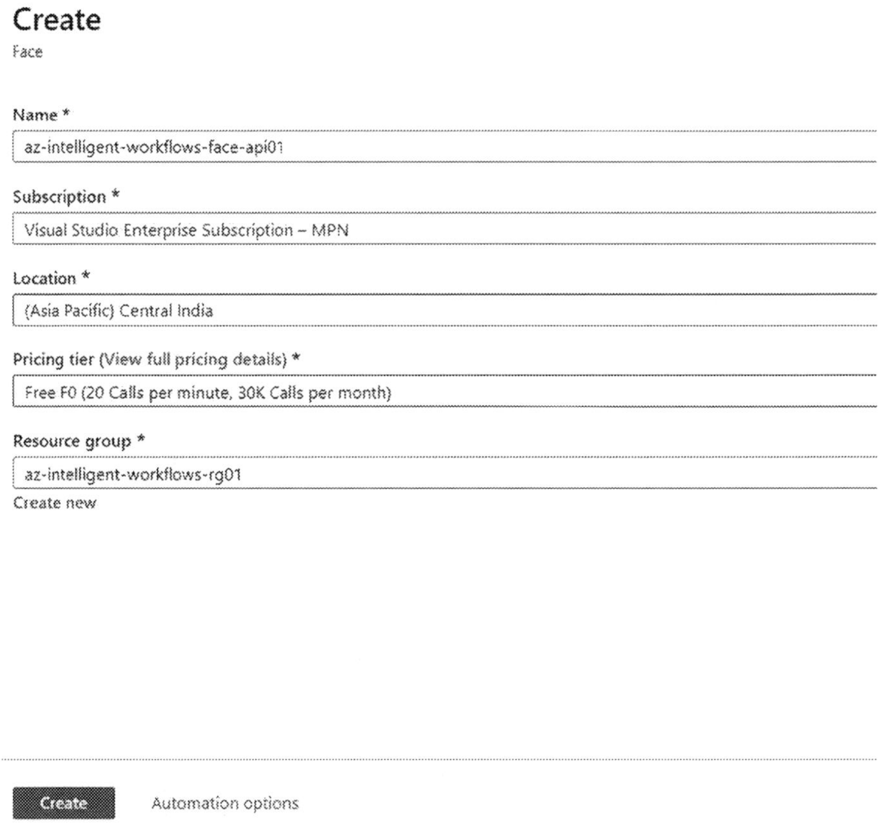

Create

Face

Name *

az-intelligent-workflows-face-api01

Subscription *

Visual Studio Enterprise Subscription – MPN

Location *

(Asia Pacific) Central India

Pricing tier (View full pricing details) *

Free F0 (20 Calls per minute, 30K Calls per month)

Resource group *

az-intelligent-workflows-rg01

Create new

Create   Automation options

Figure 3-27.   Setting details for the Face service

5. Navigate to the resource after successful deployment and click Keys and Endpoint as highlighted in Figure 3-28, and copy the values of KEY 1 and ENDPOINT. We will require these values when we create the Logic App.

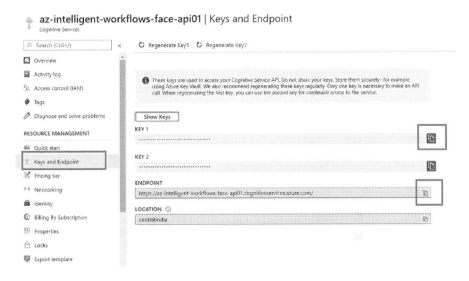

Figure 3-28. *Details for a Face resource*

Creating the Logic App

We next create the Logic App to orchestrate the process we defined in the scenario presented. Follow these steps to create the Logic App.

1. Log on to Azure Portal.

2. Click Create A Resource as shown in Figure 3-29.

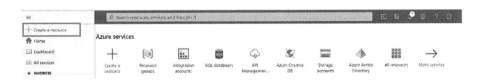

Figure 3-29. *Creating a new resource*

3. Navigate to Integration and click Logic App as shown in Figure 3-30.

Home >

New

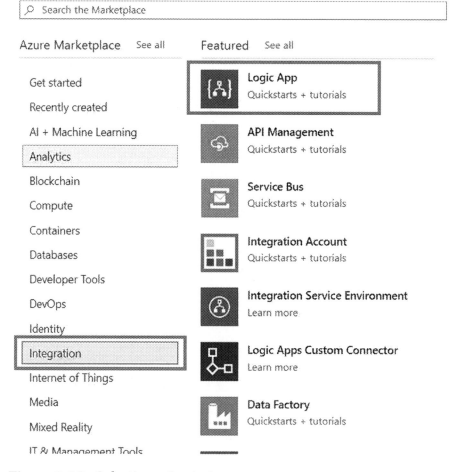

Figure 3-30. *Selecting a Logic App*

4. Enter the details as shown in Figure 3-31 and
    then click Review + Create. Once the validation is
    complete, click Create.

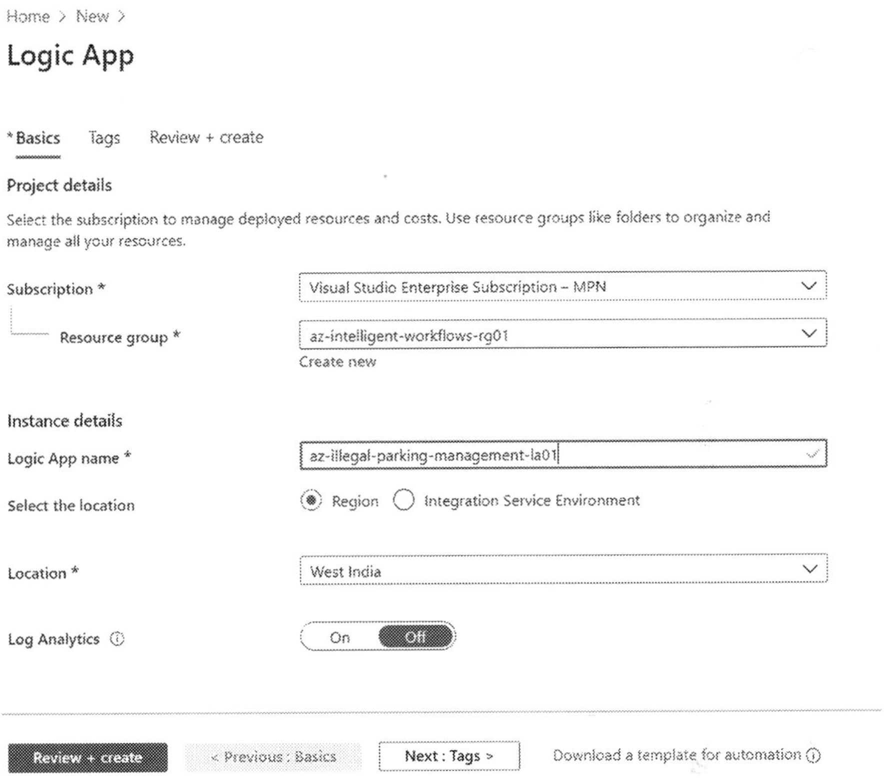

Home > New >

Logic App

* Basics   Tags   Review + create

Project details

Select the subscription to manage deployed resources and costs. Use resource groups like folders to organize and manage all your resources.

Subscription *	Visual Studio Enterprise Subscription – MPN ⌄
Resource group *	az-intelligent-workflows-rg01 ⌄
	Create new

Instance details

Logic App name *	az-illegal-parking-management-la01
Select the location	⦿ Region ◯ Integration Service Environment
Location *	West India ⌄
Log Analytics ⓘ	On **Off**

[Review + create]   < Previous : Basics   [Next : Tags >]   Download a template for automation ⓘ

Figure 3-31. *Details for Logic App*

5. The deployment for the Logic App should be quick.
    Navigate to the created Logic App.

6. You will be redirected to select a template. Click on
    the Logic App name at top left corner, as highlighted
    in Figure 3-32 to access the Logic App properties.
    We will define steps in the Logic App later in this
    section.

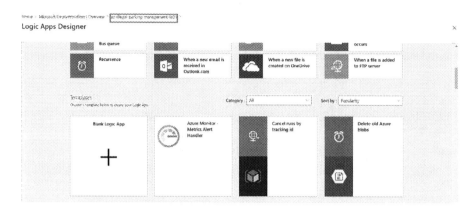

Figure 3-32. *Opening the Logic App template*

7. We next configure the Logic App to use the
    Integration Account that we created in the previous
    sections. Click Workflow Settings and select the
    Integration Account from the drop-down list, as
    shown in Figure 3-33, and click Save.

Figure 3-33. *Configuring Logic App in Integration Account*

8. We now start defining steps in the Logic App. First
    we can define the trigger for the Logic App. The
    trigger is what causes the Logic App instance to

start. In our scenario, we are going to trigger the
Logic App when a blob is created in the upload
container we created earlier. Click Logic App
Designer, highlighted in Figure 3-34, and select the
blank template to start, as displayed in Figure 3-35.

Figure 3-34. *Opening Logic App Designer*

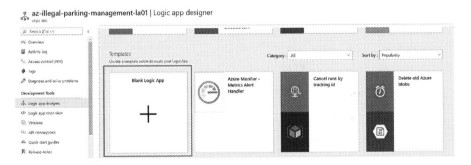

Figure 3-35. *Blank template in Logic App*

9. In the search bar, type Azure Event Grid, then and
select the trigger as shown in Figure 3-36.

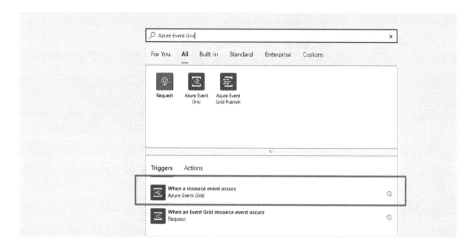

***Figure 3-36.** Azure Event Grid trigger connector*

10. Next, configure the details of the Event Grid trigger. The first step is to connect to the Azure Event Grid. There are two ways to do this. The first is to use the sign-in information for a user. The other is to create a service principal in Azure Active Directory and use it to connect to the Azure Event Grid. We will use the credentials used to log on to Azure Portal to connect to Azure Event Grid.

11. Enter the information as shown in Figure 3-37. Once done, click Add New Parameter. In the Prefix Filter field, paste /blobServices/default/containers/ upload, as highlighted in Figure 3-38. Click Save located in the top left corner of the designer.

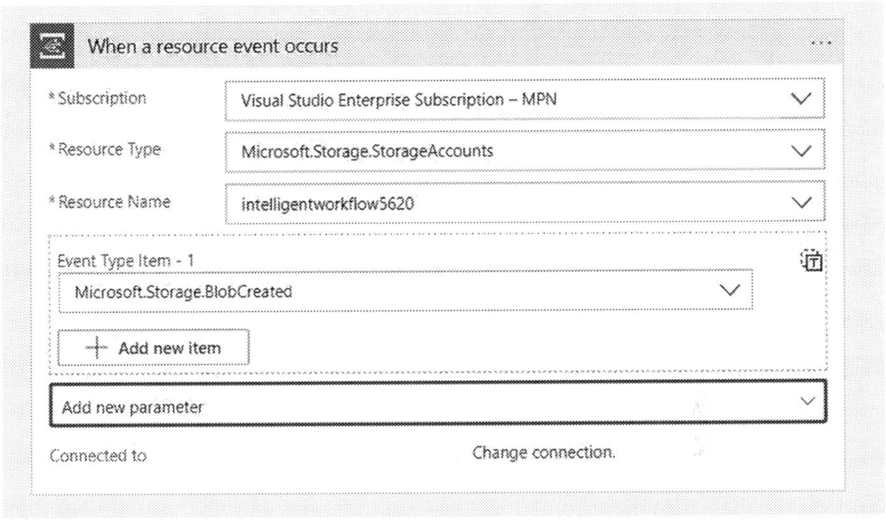

Figure 3-37. *Configuring the Event Grid connector*

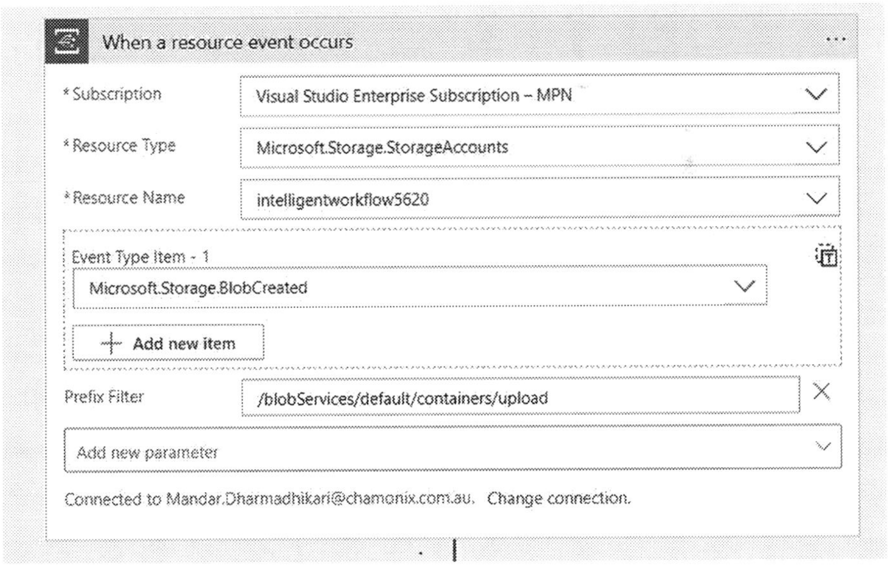

Figure 3-38. *Adding a parameter in Event Grid connector*

This allows our Logic App to trigger only when a blob is created inside the upload container.

12. Now add the connector to connect to the Face API so that we can send the image to the Face API for analysis. Click New Step and search for Face API. Select Face API, as shown in Figure 3-39. This will display all the actions available under the Face API connector. Select Detect Faces (Preview), as shown in Figure 3-40.

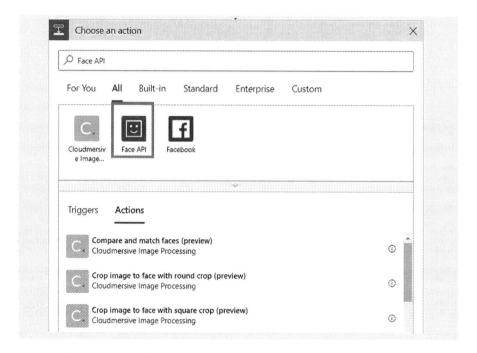

Figure 3-39. *Using the Face API connector*

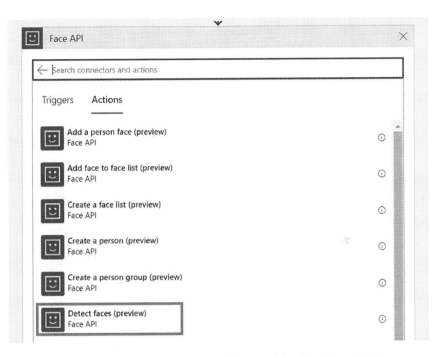

Figure 3-40. *Selecting the action to be used in the Face API connector*

13. Enter the name for the connection and the values of
     KEY1 and ENDPOINT that we captured in the last
     section while creating the Face API subscription
     (Figure 3-41). Click Create.

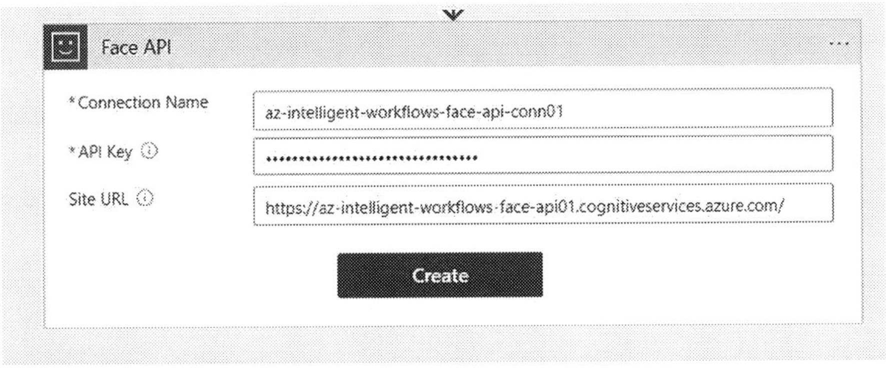

![Face API connection form showing Connection Name az-intelligent-workflows-face-api-conn01, API Key, and Site URL https://az-intelligent-workflows-face-api01.cognitiveservices.azure.com/ with a Create button]

Figure 3-41. *Connection details for Face API connector*

14. The Detect faces action expects a URL for the image. In our case, the image URL is available inside the body of the message that we get from Azure Event Grid. Click Add Dynamic Contect. That will open a Dynamic Content window. Select Expression and enter the text shown in Figure 3-42.

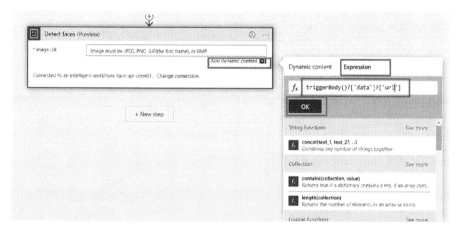

Figure 3-42. Expressions window for Face API connector

15. Click OK and save the Logic App.

16. Next we create a JSON object that will combine the response from the Face API and the image URL that we retrieved from the Azure Event Grid trigger. This object will be fed to the JSON to JSON map that we uploaded in the Integration Account. Click New Step, search for Compose, and select the Compose action as shown in Figure 3-43.

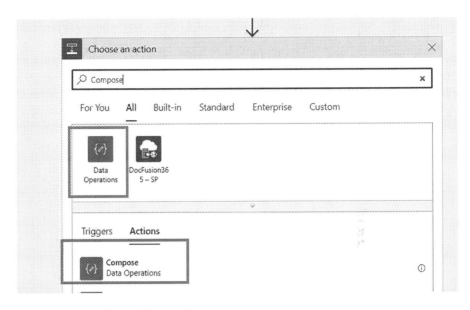

Figure 3-43. *Data Operations connector*

17. Create the JSON object as shown in Figures 3-44
and 3-45.

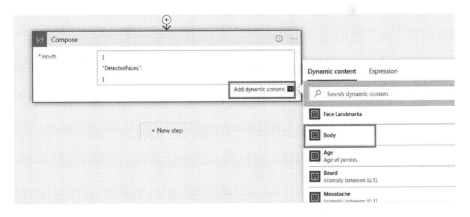

Figure 3-44. *Adding dynamic content in the Compose connector*

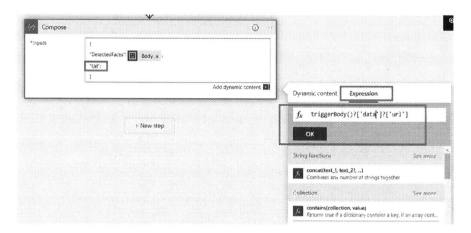

Figure 3-45. *Adding expressions in the Compose connector*

18.   Save the Logic App. The compose action should look
like Figure 3-46.

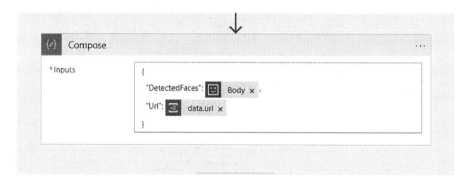

Figure 3-46. *Details of inputs for the Compose connector*

The DetectedFaces element contains the body of the
response received from the Face API and the URL is
the Blob URL from the Azure Event Grid trigger.

19. In the next step, we transform the JSON object created in previous step into the JSON object expected by the Azure function that will blur the faces in the image. Click Next Step and search for Liquid. Select Transform JSON To JSON, as highlighted in Figure 3-47.

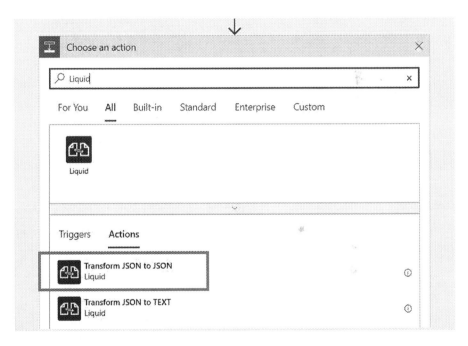

Figure 3-47. *Liquid connector*

20. Select the outputs of the compose shape as the dynamic content (Figure 3-48).

111

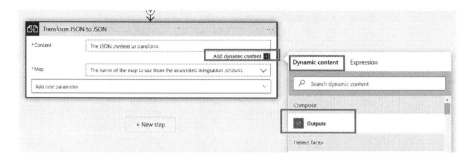

***Figure 3-48.** Entering dynamic input for the Liquid connector*

21.   Select the map name as shown in Figure 3-49. We
         linked the Logic App to the Integration Account in
         the earlier steps, so we can select the map from the
         list of the maps uploaded to the Integration Account.

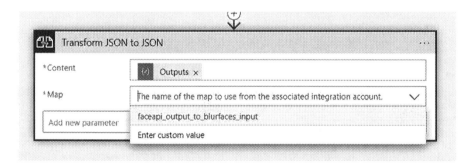

***Figure 3-49.** Map details for the Liquid connector*

The transform should look like Figure 3-50 after the
configuration.

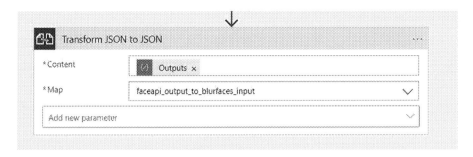

Figure 3-50. *Details for the Liquid connector*

22. Click Save to save the Logic App.

23. We will now blur the faces detected in the image. To accomplish this, we will pass the output of the transformation we created in the previous step to a HTTP triggered Azure function. Click Next Step and search for Azure Function. Click Choose An Azure Function (Figure 3-51).

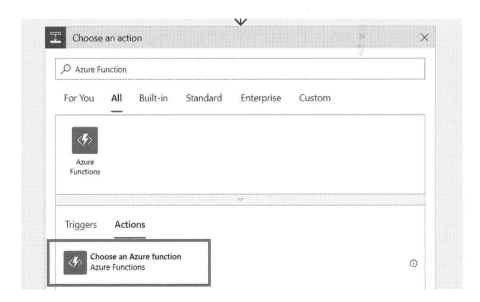

Figure 3-51. *Azure Function Liquid connector*

113

24.   Select the az-blur-faces-af01 Azure Functions app
        that we created earlier, as shown in Figure 3-52.

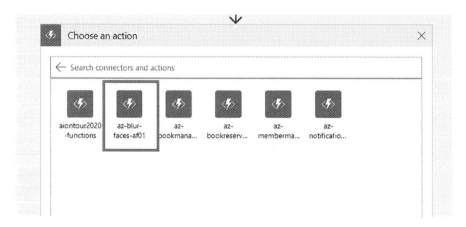

Figure 3-52. *Azure function created*

25.   Next, select the BlurFaces Azure function
        (Figure 3-53).

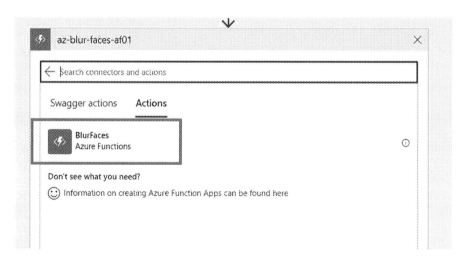

Figure 3-53. *Creating the BlurFaces Azure function Connector*

26.   Pass the output of the previous transformation action
as the Request Body, as depicted in Figure 3-54.

Figure 3-54. *Adding content to the Azure Function connector*

27.   Add the Method and Headers from the Add New
Parameter setting and configure them as shown in
Figure 3-55. Note that the value for x-functions-key
should be copied from the Azure function that we
deployed earlier.

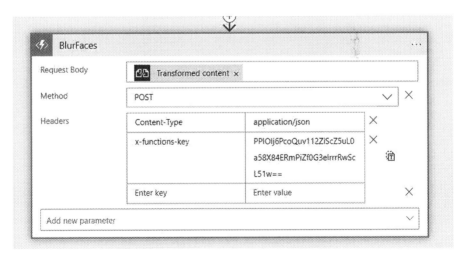

Figure 3-55. *Adding details for the Azure Function connector*

28. Click Save to save the Logic App.

29. The last step in the Logic App is to create a new blob in the processed-images container that we created to store the images after face blurring. Click Next Step, search for Blob, and select Create Blob (Figure 3-56).

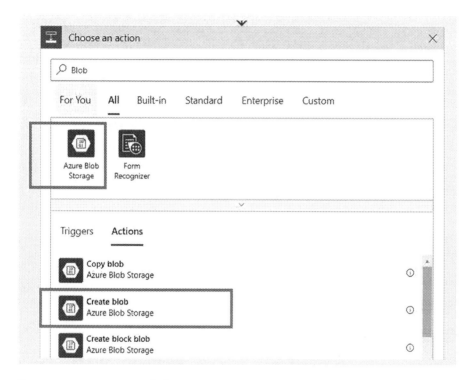

Figure 3-56. *Azure Blob connector*

30. Give a proper name to the connection, as shown in Figure 3-57, and select the storage account that we created earlier.

Figure 3-57. *Adding details for the Azure Blob connector*

31.   Configure the parameters as per Figures 3-58
through 3-61.

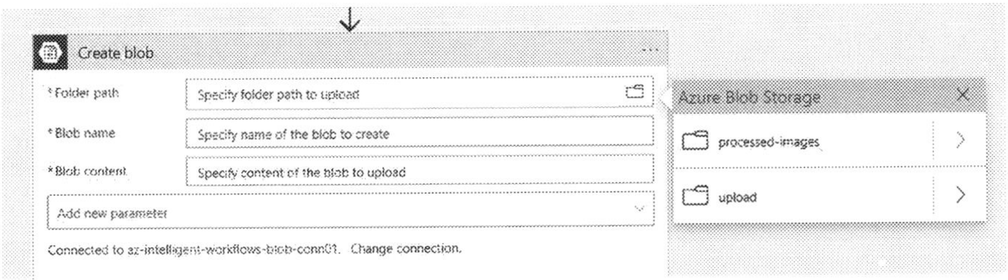

Figure 3-58. *Configuring containers for the Azure Blob
connector*

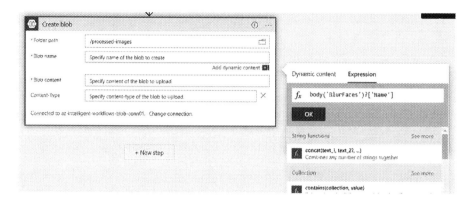

Figure 3-59. *Adding an expression for Blob name for the Azure Blob connector*

Figure 3-60. *Adding an expression for Blob content for the Azure Blob connector*

Figure 3-61. *Adding an expression for content type for the Azure Blob connector*

32. Click Save to save the Logic App. When this step is executed, the Logic App will create a new blob in the processed-images container using the name and blurred image data from the BlurFaces Azure function.

This completes the design of the Logic App. The final Logic App should look like Figure 3-62.

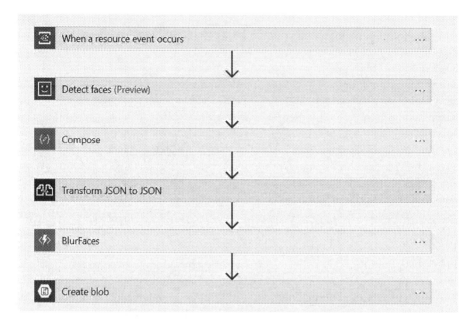

Figure 3-62. *The complete Azure Logic App workflow*

Testing the Workflow

To test the Logic App, we will upload the image to the upload container. Figure 3-63 shows the image used for testing.

Figure 3-63. *Image before testing the workflow*

The execution of the logic app is shown in Figure 3-64.

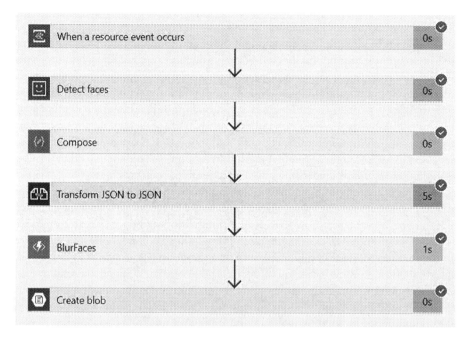

Figure 3-64. *Successful run of the Azure Logic App workflow*

The output in the processed-images container is shown in Figure 3-65.

Figure 3-65. *Image with a blurred face after testing the workflow*

It feels really awesome when everything works the first time!

Summary

In this chapter you learned how seamlessly we can achieve complex objectives using Azure Integration Services. You also learned about iPaaS services and services that are part of the iPaaS service suite. I recommend that you go through the process presented in this chapter with the given code and experience the power of Azure AI with Azure services. In the next chapter, we will explore the AI capabilities used with serverless offerings.

CHAPTER 4

AI Services with Serverless Offerings

This chapter can be considered as a continuation of last chapter, in which we used Logic Apps and the main focus was using Integration Services. This chapter focuses on using Azure AI services with the serverless computing offering Azure Functions.

Serverless Computing

Before we start, let's learn more about the term *serverless. First,* serverless does not mean no servers, but less servers. The term does imply that it consists of no servers, but that is not the case, as servers are still running the code. The underlying infrastructures are managed by a cloud service provider, so you need only focus on your functional objective and code part. The service provider automatically provisions, scales, and manages the infrastructure required to run the code. The best part is that you will be charged only for the infrastructure or resources being consumed during the execution. To learn more about serverless computing, see `https://azure.microsoft.com/en-in/overview/serverless-computing/`.

© Kasam Shaikh 2020
K. Shaikh, *Demystifying Azure AI*, https://doi.org/10.1007/978-1-4842-6219-1_4

Serverless Azure Functions

Using an event-driven development model, serverless Azure Functions, denoted by the icon shown in Figure 4-1, enable a fast-track development process. It comes with a trigger that automatically executes the code part, as a response to a defined event. It also includes bindings that help with easy integration with other Azure services.

Figure 4-1. *Azure Functions icon*

Azure Functions supports multiple widely used programming languages like .NET, Python, Java, and so on, and also comes with multiple template options for triggers, resulting in streamlined development activities. It's as simple as using the same code function implemented in a different application, all with a simple rest API call. It also supports different integrated development environments (IDEs) like Visual Studio, Visual Studio Code, and so on, to initiate, develop, build, and deploy on the cloud. You can also directly write and test the code in Azure Portal.

As far as pricing is concerned, Azure Functions uses a pay-per-execution model, which makes it one of the most recommended services in every enterprise application. To learn more about pricing, see `https://azure.microsoft.com/en-in/services/functions/#pricing`.

Infusing Azure AI

Consider you are building an application that allows users to submit product reviews that you will be listing on your web page. These reviews could be text or images.

When you allow end users to upload images through your application, along with valid product review images, there is a risk that they could upload images with irrelevant or explicit content that has no relation with your product. To avoid this problem, it's advisable to moderate the uploaded images. Imagine, though, the time and resources this manual moderation for your web application would require, and the additional expense.

In such a scenario, it would be a great benefit to have a solution in place where you just need to drop the image in a blob container that automatically moderates the image and indicates whether or not it includes inappropriate or explicit content. You could then proceed with your business functional flow.

Here we will be developing an Azure function that will perform this moderation on images automatically once they are added in Azure Blob storage. To achieve this objective, we will be using another Azure cognitive service, Content Moderator.

Content Moderator

As stated by Microsoft, "Azure Content Moderator is a cognitive service that checks text, image, and video content for material that is potentially offensive, risky, or otherwise undesirable." It detects any objectionable content in your text, image, or video file and flags it accordingly. You can then handle this flagged material and decide how to proceed. You can always use this service for centralized moderation of application content.

To learn more about the service, see `https://docs.microsoft.com/en-in/azure/cognitive-services/content-moderator/image-moderation-api`.

Along with content moderation, the service can also detect text and even faces in any given image.

Let's start with actual implementation. We will be building the low-cost, scalable, serverless solution depicted in Figure 4-2.

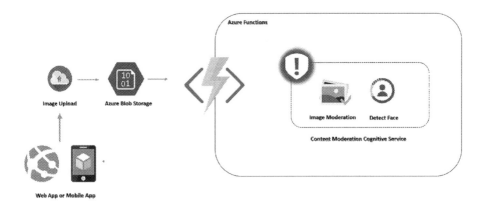

Figure 4-2. *Azure Functions with Azure AI in action*

A valid Azure subscription is required. We need to create following Azure resources.

- *Azure Blob storage:* This is used to store the product review images from users. We will be doing this using Azure Management Portal.

- *Content Moderator cognitive service:* – This is used to perform the moderation. We will be doing this using Azure Management Portal.

- *Azure Functions:* The function will be triggered automatically on image upload. We will be using the most popular IDE, Microsoft Visual Studio 2019, for the code development part.

Let's create it step by step.

Creating Azure Blob Storage

Open Azure Portal (`https://portal.azure.com`), navigate to New Resources, and search Azure Storage. Select the appropriate option, provide the required details, validate, and click Create.

Under Settings, select Access Keys, as highlighted in Figure 4-3. Copy the connection string, which you will need to configure in your Azure function. Select Containers and create a blob named `productreviewimages` with public access, as displayed in Figure 4-4. This is where all the uploaded images will be stored.

Figure 4-3. *Overview window for a storage resource*

Figure 4-4. *List of blobs in container*

Once done you are finished setting up storage, you can create the Content Moderator cognitive service.

Creating Content Moderator

In Azure Portal (`https://portal.azure.com`), go to New Resources and search for Content Moderator. Select the appropriate option, provide the required details, validate, and click Create.

You need to provide a valid name for the cognitive service, select your valid subscription, assign a location to which to deploy the service, select a resource group, and select a pricing tier.

At the time of writing, there are two pricing tiers.

- *Free F0:* 1 call per second.

- *Standard S0:* 10 calls per second.

Note   For more details about pricing tiers, visit `https://azure.`
`microsoft.com/en-us/pricing/details/cognitive-`
`services/content-moderator/`.

For this exercise, I have opted for the free tier along with the detailsshown in Figure 4-5.

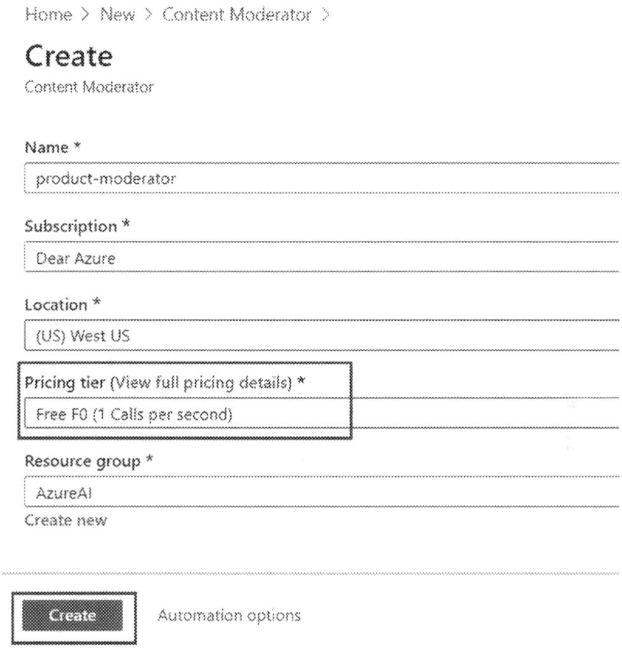

Home > New > Content Moderator >

Create
Content Moderator

Name *

product-moderator

Subscription *

Dear Azure

Location *

(US) West US

Pricing tier (View full pricing details) *

Free F0 (1 Calls per second)

Resource group *

AzureAI

Create new

Create   Automation options

Figure 4-5. *Creating Content Moderator service*

Once the service is deployed and created, under Resource
Management, navigate to Key and Endpoint (Figure 4-6). Note the
key, endpoint, and location, as this too will be configured in our Azure
function.

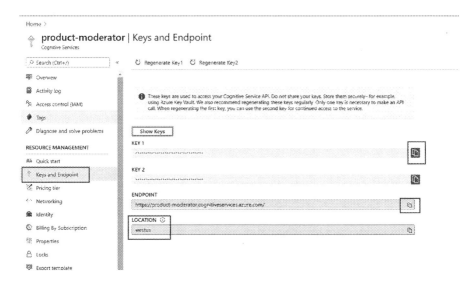

Figure 4-6. *Keys and Endpoint information*

After you have completed these steps, its time to work with Azure Functions and configure the deployed resources to meet our functional objective.

Creating Azure Function

We will be using the most popular IDE among developers, Visual Studio 2019, to creating the Azure function.

Note   Make sure you have downloaded the Azure workloads along with Visual Studio 2019, for access to the Azure templates, in our case, the Azure Functions templates.

Open Visual Studio 2019 (it is recommended that you run it as an administrator) and click Create A New Project, as shown in Figure 4-7.

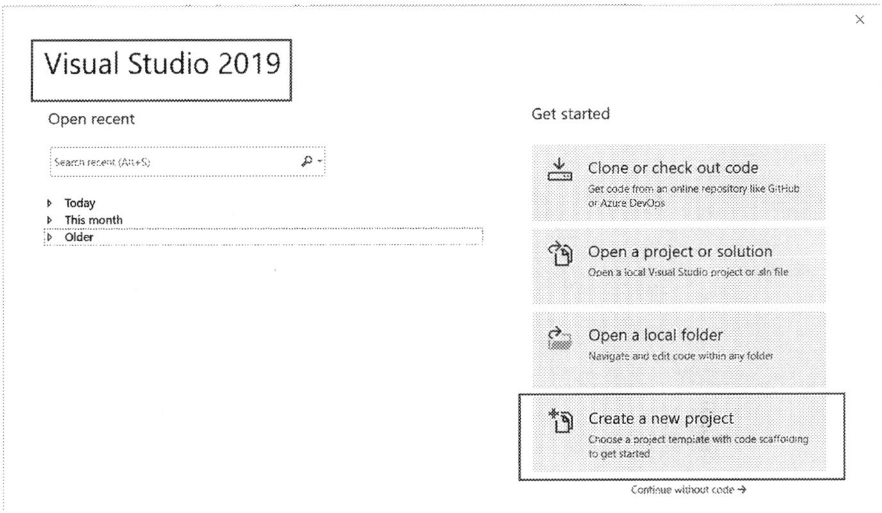

Figure 4-7. *Getting started with Visual Studio 2019*

Note   In this exercise, I am using the Visual Studio 2019 free community edition. You can use the licensed version for production-ready solutions.

Next, type Azure Functions in the search box. For Recent Project Templates, select Cloud. From the list of templates provided (Figure 4-9), select Azure Functions with C# as the language option.

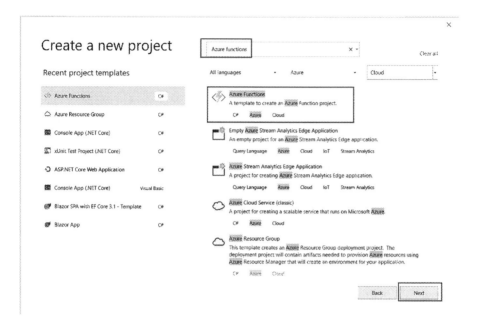

Figure 4-8. *Creating a new project in Visual Studio 2019*

Click Next to proceed.

Configure the newly created project with a name and location. Click Create to proceed. In the example shown in Figure 4-9, I have given the project the name ProductReviewModeration.

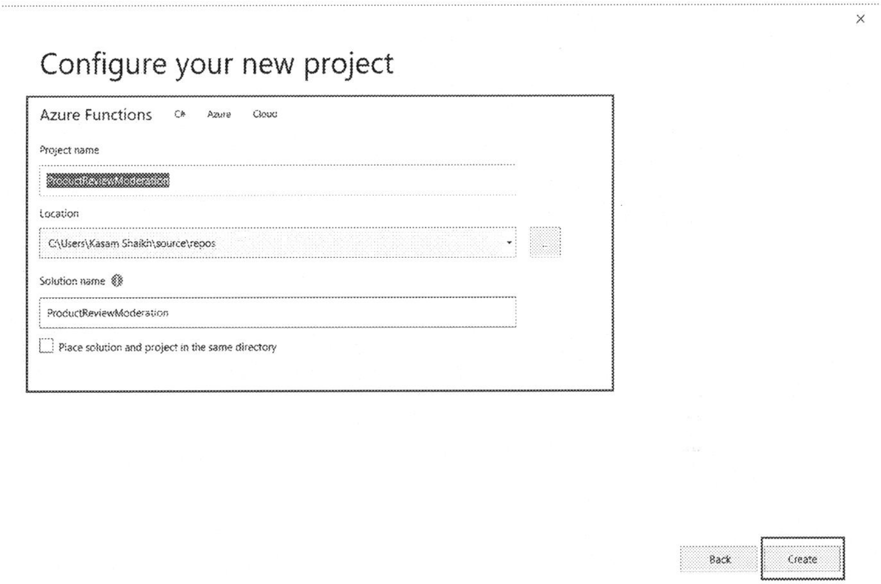

×

Configure your new project

Azure Functions   C#   Azure   Cloud

Project name

ProductReviewModeration

Location

C:\Users\Kasam Shaikh\source\repos

Solution name

ProductReviewModeration

☐ Place solution and project in the same directory

Back   Create

Figure 4-9. *Configuring a new project in Visual Studio 2019*

Now we can configure the Azure Functions application. After clicking Create in the preceding step, you will be presented with the following options.

- *Azure Function Runtime Version:* At the time of writing, there are three runtime options, displayed in Figure 4-10.

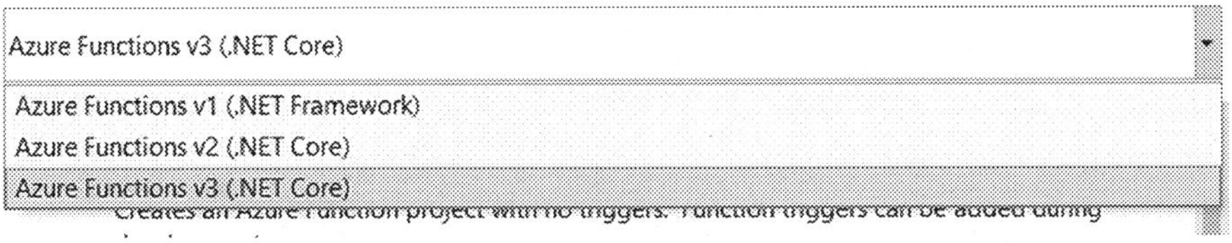

Azure Functions v3 (.NET Core)

Azure Functions v1 (.NET Framework)
Azure Functions v2 (.NET Core)
Azure Functions v3 (.NET Core)

Creates an Azure Function project with no triggers. Function triggers can be added during

Figure 4-10. *Options to select the Runtime in Visual Studio 2019*

We will select v3, which is the latest version, as the runtime. To learn more about Azure Functions runtime versions, see `https://docs.microsoft.com/en-us/azure/azure-functions/functions-versions`.

Triggers: This is what causes the function run. It's a definition for how the function will be invoked. Every function must have just one trigger. The data associated with this trigger serve as a payload for the function. For more details on the concept of triggers, see `https://docs.microsoft.com/en-us/azure/azure-functions/functions-triggers-bindings`.

For this exercise, I will be selecting Blob trigger.

- Associated Storage Accounts: As we need to moderate the product review images, we need to store those images. That will trigger the Azure function and moderate the images for further processing. To store these images, we have created a storage account and blob. We need to configure the storage details here.

From the Storage Account drop-down list, select Browse, as shown in Figure 4-11.

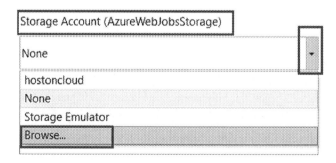

Figure 4-11. *Configuration options for storage in Visual Studio 2019*

This opens the window to select your subscription and a list of existing storage account under the subscription, to associate with the Azure Functions application. You can also create a new storage account using the link mentioned in the window.

I will be selecting the storage account we created in preceding steps, as shown in Figure 4-12.

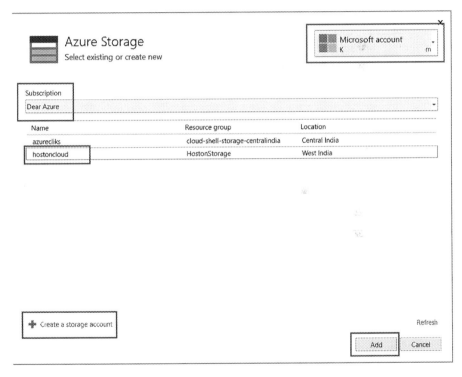

Figure 4-12. *Selecting a storage account in Visual Studio 2019*

Click Add to proceed.

Next, provide a valid name for Connection String Setting Name. For the Path value, add the blob name we created in the preceding steps (Figure 4-13).

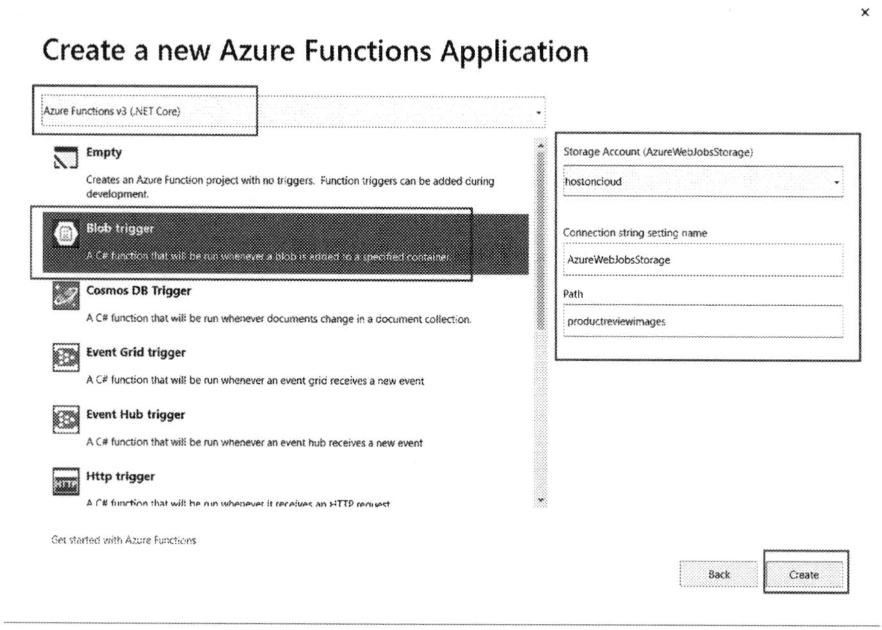

Figure 4-13. *Selecting a template in Visual Studio 2019*

This will confirm that at the given path under the associated Azure storage account, if any images get added, Azure Functions is invoked to run.

Click Create to create the function. The files created are shown in Solution Explorer in Figure 4-14.

Figure 4-14. *Files created in Solution Explorer*

Rename the function class file with any valid function name. To verify, everything is working, open the function file, and place the breakpoint under the Run method. Build and run the function, and wait for the host to start, as shown in Figure 4-15.

```
Azure Functions Core Tools (3.0.2630 Commit hash: beec61496e1c5de8aa4ba38d1884f7b48233a7ab)
Function Runtime Version: 3.0.13901.0
[26-06-2020 22:46:09] Building host: startup suppressed: 'False', configuration suppressed: 'False', startup operation i
d: 'fc90753f-c440-464c-9eb7-6698528f581a'
[26-06-2020 22:46:09] Reading host configuration file '                           \ProductReviewModeration\Produc
tReviewModeration\bin\Debug\netcoreapp3.1\host.json'
[26-06-2020 22:46:09] Host configuration file read:
[26-06-2020 22:46:09] {
[26-06-2020 22:46:09]   "version": "2.0",
[26-06-2020 22:46:09]   "logging": {
[26-06-2020 22:46:09]     "applicationInsights": {
[26-06-2020 22:46:09]       "samplingExcludedTypes": "Request",
[26-06-2020 22:46:09]       "samplingSettings": {
[26-06-2020 22:46:09]         "isEnabled": true
[26-06-2020 22:46:09]       }
[26-06-2020 22:46:09]     }
[26-06-2020 22:46:09]   }
```

Figure 4-15. *Running the application*

Next, upload any image to the blob container. You can directly upload the image from Azure Portal or use Azure Storage Explorer, the recommended free tool to manage Azure storage accounts. To download and learn more about the tool, visit `https://azure.microsoft.com/en-us/features/storage-explorer/`.

I use Azure Storage Explorer here, as shown in Figure 4-16, and upload an image. This action should now invoke our Azure function.

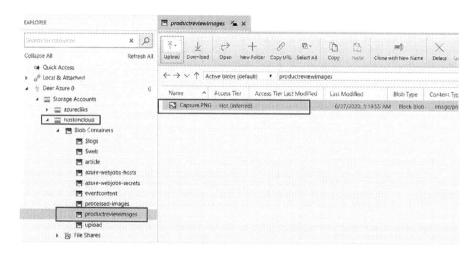

Figure 4-16. *Azure Storage Explorer*

Checking the break point, we can see the details of the uploaded image, as highlighted in Figure 4-17.

Figure 4-17. *Code at debugging point*

It's running absolutely fine. Next, will add code to infuse the Content Moderator service into our Azure function. First we will be adding the service endpoint and access key into the code. The best way to do that is adding it as key value entry in the `local.setting.json` application config file.

We have added the key name `Moderator_API_Endpoint` for endpoint, with the value of the URL that needs to be called to perform the operation, and `Moderator_API_Subscription_Key` with key value as the access key of the Content Moderator service we copied in earlier steps (Figure 4-18).

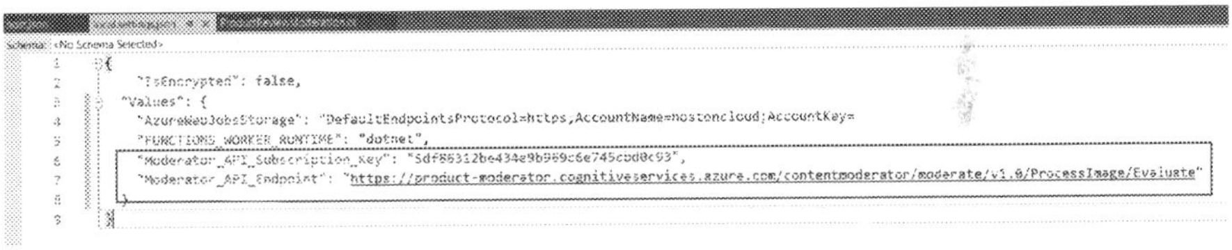

***Figure 4-18.** Configuration settings in Visual Studio 2019*

You can find all the reference API URLs at `https://westus2.dev.cognitive.microsoft.com/docs/services/57cf753a3f9b070c105bd2c1/operations/57cf753a3f9b070868a1f66c/console`. That link, shown in Figure 4-19, will detail all possible operations the service can perform. Just provide the relevant information about the service you created, like the service resource name and key, and it will present you with the request URL or endpoint you should be using in your application.

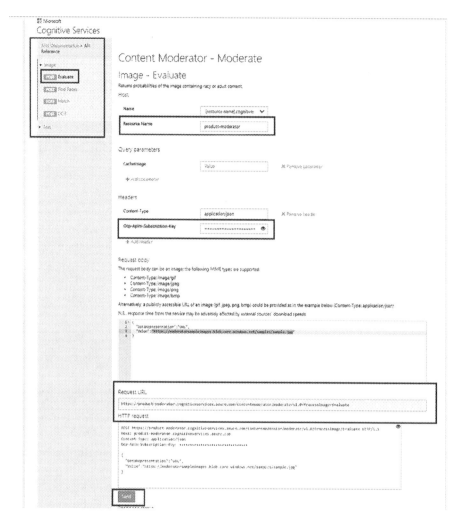

Figure 4-19. *API console for Content Moderator service*

You can also test few sample images by passing the Image URL using this API console.

Once you have added the required keys in the config file, let's add the code to call the image and call the service.

Copy and paste the following code in your function class file.

```csharp
static async Task<bool> CallContentModeratorAPI(Stream
image,string name)
    {
        string contentType = GetConentType(name);
        using (var memoryStream = new MemoryStream())
        {
            image.Position = 0;
            image.CopyTo(memoryStream);
            memoryStream.Position = 0;

            using (var client = new HttpClient())
            {
                var content = new StreamContent(memoryStream);
                var url = Environment.GetEnvironmentVariable
                ("Moderator_API_Endpoint");
                client.DefaultRequestHeaders.Add("Ocp-Apim-
                Subscription-Key", Environment.GetEnviron
                mentVariable("Moderator_API_Subscription_
                Key"));
                content.Headers.ContentType = new MediaType
                HeaderValue(contentType);
                var httpResponse = await client.
                PostAsync(url, content);

                if (httpResponse.StatusCode ==
                HttpStatusCode.OK)
                {
                    Task<string> task = Task.
                    Run<string>(async () =>
                    await httpResponse.Content.
                    ReadAsStringAsync());
                    string result = task.Result;
```

```
                    if (String.IsNullOrEmpty(result))
                    {
                        return false;
                    }
                    else
                    {
                        dynamic json = JValue.
                        Parse(result);
                        return (!((bool)json.
                        IsImageAdultClassified || (bool)
                        json.IsImageRacyClassified));
                    }

                }
            }
        }

        return false;
    }
```

Then call this method in your main function.

```
public static async Task Run([BlobTrigger("productreviewimag
es/{name}", Connection = "AzureWebJobsStorage")]Stream myBlob,
string name, ILogger log)
        {
            log.LogInformation($"C# Blob trigger function
            Processed blob\n Name:{name} \n Size: {myBlob.
            Length} Bytes");

            // Function to Moderate the Image added
            bool result = await CallContentModeratorAPI(myBlob,
            name);
```

```
//Log Response
log.LogInformation("Product Review Image - " +
(result ? "Approved" : "Denied"));
}
```

Now your file will look like that shown in Figure 4-20.

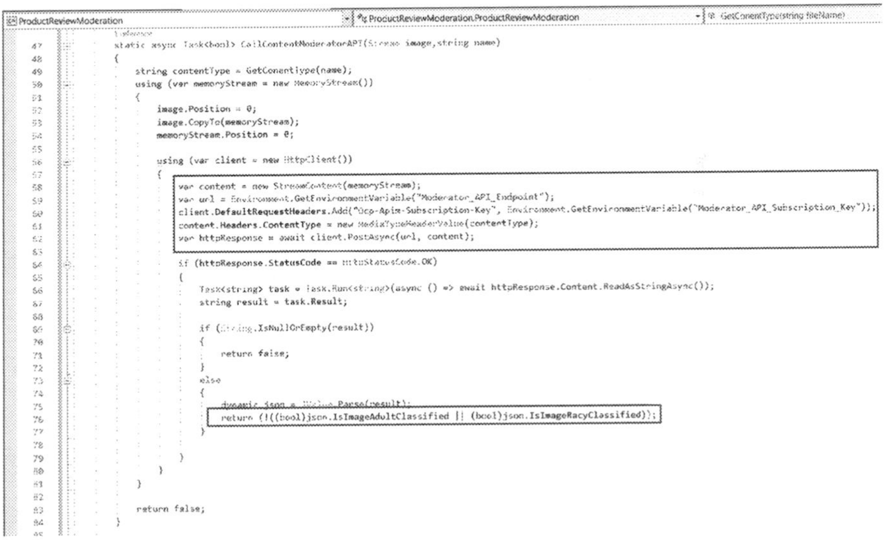

Figure 4-20. *Azure function method code view in Visual Studio 2019*

The Run method will look like Figure 4-21.

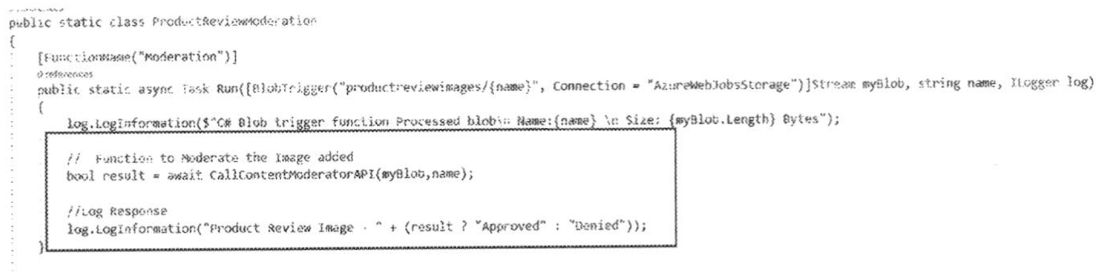

Figure 4-21. *Azure function code view in Visual Studio 2019*

Now it is time to test the function. Run the application, and add the image to the blob container.

I have used the sample image provided by Microsoft in the previously mentioned API console, at `https://moderatorsampleimages.blob.core.windows.net/samples/sample.jpg`. Download the image from that URL, or use any of your images, and upload it to the container, as shown in Figure 4-22.

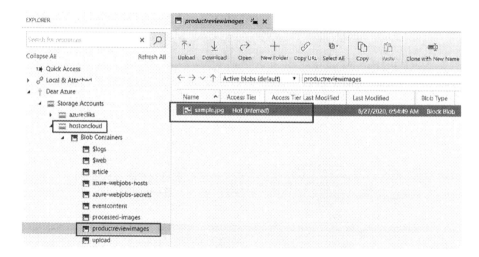

Figure 4-22. *Azure Storage Explorer*

This will trigger the Azure function, and the result will be logged, as can be seen in Figure 4-23.

```
[27-06-2020 01:27:04] Starting JobHost
[27-06-2020 01:27:04] Starting Host (HostId=desktopn6i4bqk-1505796546, InstanceId=48209a37-28c1-4005-a47f-771e5d39a8e
Version=3.0.13901.0, ProcessId=27852, AppDomainId=1, InDebugMode=False, InDiagnosticMode=False, FunctionsExtensionVer
n=(null))
[27-06-2020 01:27:04] Loading functions metadata
[27-06-2020 01:27:04] 1 functions loaded
[27-06-2020 01:27:04] Generating 1 job function(s)
[27-06-2020 01:27:04] Found the following functions:
[27-06-2020 01:27:04] ProductReviewModeration.ProductReviewModeration.Run
[27-06-2020 01:27:04]
[27-06-2020 01:27:05] Initializing function HTTP routes
[27-06-2020 01:27:05] No HTTP routes mapped
[27-06-2020 01:27:05]
[27-06-2020 01:27:05] Host initialized (620ms)
[27-06-2020 01:27:05] Host started (692ms)
[27-06-2020 01:27:05] Job host started
Hosting environment: Production
Content root path: C:\Users\Kasam Shaikh\source\repos\ProductReviewModeration\ProductReviewModeration\bin\Debug\netco
pp3.1
Now listening on: http://0.0.0.0:7071
Application started. Press Ctrl+C to shut down.
[27-06-2020 01:27:05] Executing 'Moderation' (Reason='New blob detected: productreviewimages/sample.jpg', Id=d50b8250
61-4aaa-adf9-02879b57115a)
[27-06-2020 01:27:05] C# Blob trigger function Processed blob
Name:sample.jpg
Size: 273405 Bytes
[27-06-2020 01:27:08] Product Review Image - Approved
[27-06-2020 01:27:08] Executed 'Moderation' (Succeeded, Id=d50b8250-6051-4aaa-adf9-02879b57115a)
[27-06-2020 01:27:10] Host lock lease acquired by instance ID '00000000000000000000000ECC64A81'.
```

Figure 4-23. *Functions log in Visual Studio 2019*

Now, add another image using Azure Storage Explorer, as depicted in Figure 4-24.

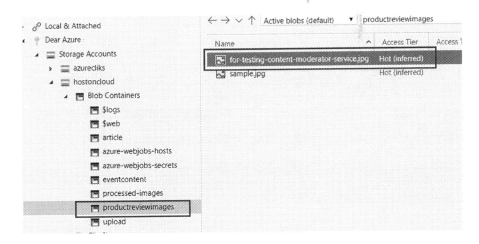

Figure 4-24. *Azure Storage Explorer*

Now check the log, as highlighted in Figure 4-25.

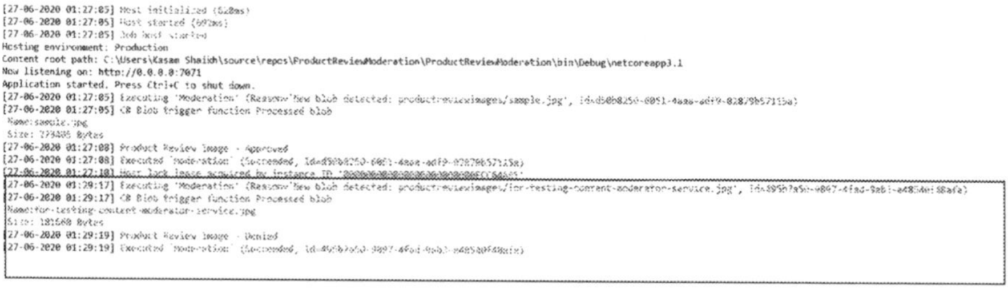

Figure 4-25. Functions log in Visual Studio 2019

Notice in Figure 4-25 that the image is as denied.

Note I have uploaded the image that would not pass the Content Moderator evaluation test for demo purposes only.

Now you have seen how seamlessly we added the Azure AI services into Azure Functions, and met our objective to efficiently moderate image content.

You can also use the Content Moderator service to find human faces in any given image. I suggest this as an exercise for learning purposes.

As a hint, you can use the same access key, and URL as `https://westus2.dev.cognitive.microsoft.com/docs/services/57cf753a3f9b070c105bd2c1/operations/57cf753a3f9b070868a1f66a`.

If you find the faces, you can set the results set to be Yes; if there are no faces, then set it to No. Feel free to share your experience with me once you perform this exercise.

What You Can Do

As you saw in the workflow in Chapter 3, we triggered our Logic Apps on an image being added to Azure Blob storage. We then passed the image to the Face Detect API to get the faces and later passed the face coordinates to Azure Functions to perform a blurring process. Here, in place of the Face Detect API, we can also directly call the Face Detect service or Content Moderator service inside our Azure function. You can change your workflow to have this detection in Azure Functions.

You can also now directly publish this code from Visual Studio 2019 to Azure, and make the application live..

A Must Read

I advise you to go through an open project on Azure Functions Extensions for Cognitive Services (Figure 4-26), a collection of Azure Functions bindings that greatly simplify working with Microsoft Cognitive Services. This project was developed by Josh Carlisle, a Microsoft MVP in Azure, innovator, architect, and cloud advocate based in Raleigh, North Carolina. The extension is a set of custom Azure Functions bindings for Azure Cognitive Services.

You can explore this project on GitHub at `https://github.com/joshdcar/azure-functions-extensions-cognitive-services`.

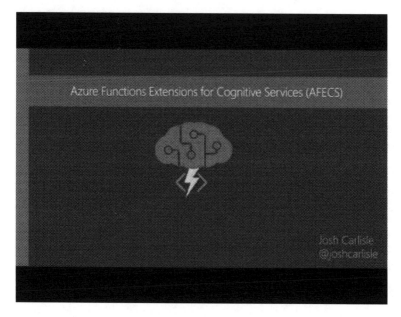

Figure 4-26. *Azure Functions Extensions for Cognitive Services on GitHub*

Summary

By now, you are aware about the power of AI capabilities and simplicity in its implementation with Azure services. This chapter presented how you can work with different AI services with the serverless offering Azure Functions. I also went through the steps to create an Azure function with a Blob trigger using Visual Studio 2019 as the IDE. Along with Cognitive Services and Azure Functions, we also looked at Azure Storage Explorer, which is used to manage the storage accounts. In the next chapter, we cover working with AI services with a low code platform.

CHAPTER 5

AI with Low Code

In the last chapter you saw how seamlessly you can use the power of
Azure Cognitive Services with serverless offerings of Azure Functions. This
chapter presents you with Azure AI capabilities offered by Microsoft Azure
with a low-code platform. Here, the chapter focuses on what and how
these amazing smart services can be used in Microsoft Power Automate.

Low-Code Platform

There are many definitions for this term, but the best and easiest to
understand that I found is this: "A low-code development platform
is software that provides a development environment used to create
application software through graphical user interfaces and configuration
instead of traditional hand-coded computer programming." In simpler
terms, it is application development approach with more graphic user
interace (GUI) and less (low) coding.

It is also used for automating tedious business workflows by allowing
you to draw a flowchart. The code gets generated automatically, reducing
traditional programming efforts.

© Kasam Shaikh 2020
K. Shaikh, *Demystifying Azure AI*, https://doi.org/10.1007/978-1-4842-6219-1_5

Why Choose Low Code

As it involves minimal code efforts, many resources can contribute in the overall application development phase. Not only is the end result achieved much faster, but the complexity of development is also reduced. The most important reason to choose low code is that it provides higher productivity and lower costs.

Power Platform

Before diving into work with Power Automate, lets first briefly go through Power Platform. Power Platform in simpler terms, is a set of four amazing products.

Power Apps

PowerApps, denoted by the icon in Figure 5-1, is a low-code development platform from Microsoft that enables you to build rich mobile and web applications seamlessly with higher productivity. It empowers developers to leverage low-code capabilities in achieving the application functionality with speedy delivery maintaining the agility of organizations.

Figure 5-1. *Icon used for Power Apps*

Power Automate

Another product with low-code capabilities, Power Automate (Figure 5-2 shows its icon) enables you to create automated business workflows between applications and services. It empowers developers to leverage low-code capabilities in automating repetitive business processes such as notifications, data collections, and business-related decision approvals.

Figure 5-2. *Icon used for Power Automate*

As mentioned earlier, this chapter will present more details with respect to the use of Azure AI services with Power Automate.

Power BI

Power BI, denoted by the icon shown in Figure 5-3, is a business analytics service that delivers insights for analyzing data. It enables you to create reports, create dashboards with different data sources, and present insight through visuals. It allows an organization to focus on analyzing the data rather than spending time in managing them. You can showcase the business data in the most viewable format.

Figure 5-3. *Icon used for Power BI*

Power Virtual Agents

Power Virtual Agents, denoted by the icon shown in Figure 5-4, enables you to build smart chat bots with GUIs without code. You don't need to be a data scientist or have bot development skills to use this product. It's an excellent way to generate futuristic intelligent conversational bots in no time.

Figure 5-4. *Icon used for Power Virtual Agents*

I could write an entire book on the subject of these amazing products. For now, though, let's focus on the chapter scope.

Note   If you are planning to dive in further with Power Platform, you should start with Power Platform Fundamentals at https:// docs.microsoft.com/en-us/learn/paths/power-plat- fundamentals/.

Working with Power Automate

To start working with Power Automate, you don't need to install or download any tools or software. You can use and create the smart business workflows all via browser. Power Automate does come with a web portal presenting a GUI to build the workflows.

Open https://flow.microsoft.com/ (Figure 5-5).

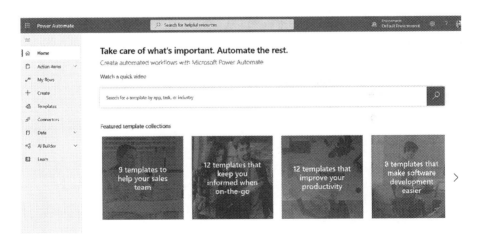

Figure 5-5. *Home page of Power Automate web portal*

As a prerequisite, you need to register with Power Automate to create and manage the workflows. You should sign up with your work account to leverage the power of the product. Alternatively, you can also sign up for a free trial with your personal email account, but then use of many of the features, like premium connectors, team flows, and more, is restricted. We will cover this later in this chapter.

Note   For this chapter, I have signed up with my personal account. You need to have a licenced version for production-ready workflows. For more details visit `https://flow.microsoft.com/en-us/pricing/`.

Previously known as Microsoft Flow, Power Automate is very similar to Azure Logic Apps. It comes with the same actions, triggers, and connectors. At the time of writing, there are more than 325 connectors available. It places greater emphasis on business-related connectors like Salesforce, Office 365, SharePoint, MS Teams, and connectors related to Approvals workflows.

Once you open the portal with a valid registration, several options are available in the left corner of the screen, as shown in Figure 5-6.

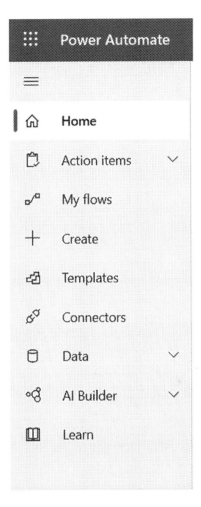

Figure 5-6. *Menu options available in Power Automate Web portal*

These options help you start building workflows, based on your business requirements.

- *Action Items:* This presents the nature of the workflow; for example, whether its an approval-based workflow or business workflow. It involves premium connectors, and hence needs an account with a valid license.

- *My Flows:* Here are all the workflows you have created categorized by type and ownership. Except for individually created workflows, all other types and ownerships require a valid license.

- *Create:* This option is where you start creating new flows. It comes with three options. You can either start from scratch, use preapproved templates, or start with the available connectors.

- *Templates:* This option provides prebuilt approved workflows, ready to use with minimal customization and configurations.

- *Connectors:* You can select from more than 300 connectors to start your workflows, as per the business requirements or use case.

- *Data:* This enters the picture when you work with Power Apps. It also provides options to create custom connectors and enables you to extend your workflows. Here you need an account with a valid license.

- *AI Builder:* This feature in Power Platform enables you to add AI capabilities to your Power Apps and workflow. It's a solution that enables you to infuse intelligence in to your apps and predicts outcomes, resulting in improved business performance, all without writing code.

Again, this is a vast and an interesting topic related to Power Platform. You can work with AI Builder when your flow communicates with Common Data Services or an enhancement call from Power Apps. You will encounter these terms while working with Power Apps and Power Automate, in short Power Platform. I do not go further with this topic, as I am more interested here in covering the use of Azure Cognitive Services with Power Automate.

Azure AI Services

As mentioned in Chapter 3, Azure Cognitive Services are provided to the developers as RESTful APIs. All of these can be used inside Power Automate to create intelligent business workflows. Let's see what Cognitive Services connectors are readily available to use.

Open the portal and click the Connectors option from the menu on the left. In the search box, type the name of the connector type your are looking for. In our case, type Azure, as shown in Figure 5-7.

Figure 5-7. *Connectors listed for Azure*

Notice in Figure 5-7 that all Azure-related connectors like Azure Blob, Azure VM, Azure Automation, and so on, except for Azure AD, are marked as premium connectors. Luckily, this is not the case with Azure AI service connectors.

At the time of writing, the following connectors for Azure Cognitive Services are available in the Power Automate Connectors blade.

- Bing Search

- Computer Vision

- Custom Vision

- Face Detection

- LUIS

- Text Analytics

- QnA Maker (Preview)

More services could be added in the future. We will be looking into a few of the services here: Face Detection, Computer Vision, and Text Analytics.

Face Detection

The Face cognitive service is used to detect a person's face or recognize a person's face in any given image. Along with the face coordinates, it provides the gender, age, emotions, and a few other attributes related to image.

Creating Face Service

To create a Face service resource, open Azure Portal (`https://portal.azure.com/`). Click New Resource, and type Face. Press Enter. You will presented with the service page shown in Figure 5-8. Click Create to proceed.

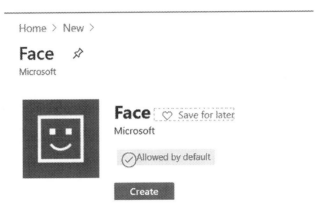

Figure 5-8. *Azure Face service main page*

It presents you with a blade, as shown in Figure 5-9, to enter few mandatory details. There are fields for Name, Subscription, Location, Pricing Tier, and Resource Group. Provide the details and click Create. Once the information is validated, this creates the resource.

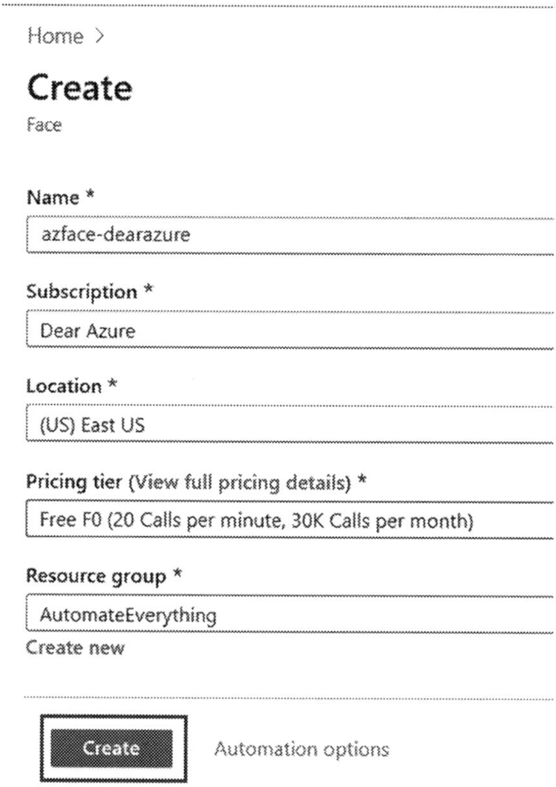

Home >

Create
Face

Name *

azface-dearazure

Subscription *

Dear Azure

Location *

(US) East US

Pricing tier (View full pricing details) *

Free F0 (20 Calls per minute, 30K Calls per month)

Resource group *

AutomateEverything

Create new

Create   Automation options

Figure 5-9. *Creating a service in Azure Portal*

Once the service is created, go to the resource page. In the Resource Management section, select Keys and Endpoint, highlighted in Figure 5-10.

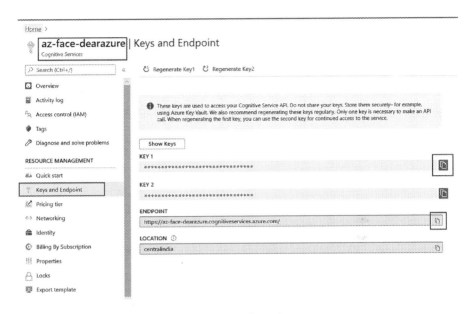

Figure 5-10. *Sections with Keys and Endpoint*

Copy the values for Resource Name, either Key 1 or Key 2, and the Endpoint URL. We will be using these values later in our Power Automate workflow.

Now that we have created the Face Detection service, let's use it in our Power Automate flow. Consider, the same use case we created in Chapter 3. Once an image is uploaded to the configured blob, Logic App is triggered. Here we will not create the workflow again, but instead build it to trigger manually. Let's go through the process.

Begin by opening the Power Automate portal. From the left menu, select Create. From the three options for creating a flow, select Start From Blank. This will allow us to create a custom flow to meet our requirement (Figure 5-11).

Figure 5-11. *Options for types of flow*

There are five options to choose from.

- *Automated Flow:* It gets triggered by an event.

- *Instant Flow:* This could be triggered as required. We will be using this flow.

- *Schedule Flow:* The trigger can be scheduled as required.

- *UI Flow:* Record the process in the UI.

- *Business Process Flow:* Guides users with a defined business process.

Click Instant Flow, as highlighted in Figure 5-11, to start creating the flows. You will be prompted with a window to select or configure how the flow will be initiated. It will list all trigger options available, including SharePoint, PowerApps, OneDrive, and so on.

Along with all the other options, there is one option that enables you to manually trigger the flow. Select this option. The Create button will initially be disabled, and will be enabled only when you select any trigger option from the list (Figure 5-12).

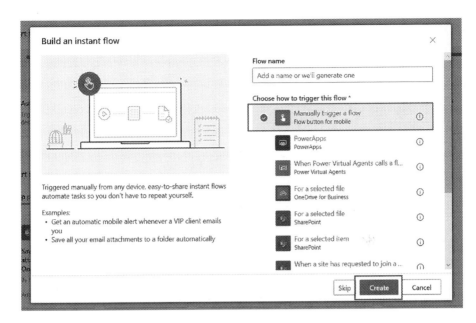

Figure 5-12. *Options to trigger flow*

Click Create to proceed. This will open the designer screen for creating the workflows. As we have selected manual trigger options, the screen includes the respective connector.

First let's name the workflow. In this example, shown in Figure 5-13, I have renamed the flow from Untitled to AI with Low Code – Face API. Appropriately naming the workflows is not necessary, but it is recommended. It should be considered best practice to helps in further management of the flows.

Figure 5-13. *Connector to manually trigger the flow*

In the trigger connector, you have different options to pass on the data to the next connector for performing an action. Click + Add An Input to see the multiple options to pass the data. Now, in our case the next connector will be for the Face Detection service, and it needs the URL for the data to work on.

Select the Text option (Figure 5-14) and provide the blob image URL as text. Consider that we have the preceding trigger connector as Azure Blob, and as the image is uploaded it will trigger the flow.

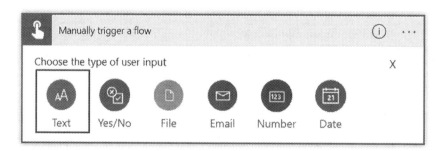

Figure 5-14. *User input types for the trigger connector*

Note   To avoid the repetition of steps, I introduced a manual trigger option here. To replicate the functional flow, though, use the blob URL as text.

166

Why not directly pass the file using File as the input type? This manual trigger connector provides the file content and not the file URL, which is required by Face Connector.

Once you have selected the input type, click Save to save the workflow. Again it is best practice to always save the workflow and click Flow Checker to validate that there are no errors or issues with the flow. When you click Save, though, it will give you an error message, as the flow as no action attached to it. To save successfully, a workflow should contain at least one trigger and one action.

To add the next connector to perform an action on the provided data, click + New Step, at the bottom of the connector, as shown in Figure 5-15.

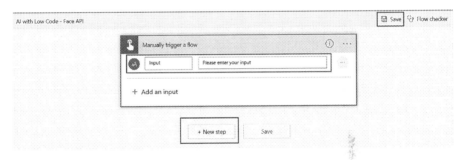

Figure 5-15. *Manual trigger with details*

This will open a window that allows you to select from all available connectors. Type Face in search box to display the Face Detection connector. You will also see the list of actions available with the connector (Figure 5-16).

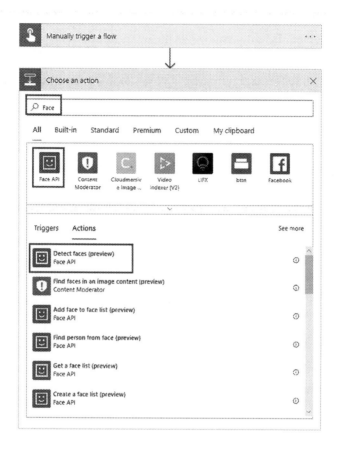

Figure 5-16. *Face connector*

Select the Detect Faces (Preview) action. Although it's in preview, it can be used for learning purposes.

Once the action is selected, you will have to supply the appropriate details pertaining to the Face cognitive service. In earlier steps for creating the Face resource, we copied the connection name, API key, and endpoint. Those same details need to be provided here, as shown in Figure 5-17.

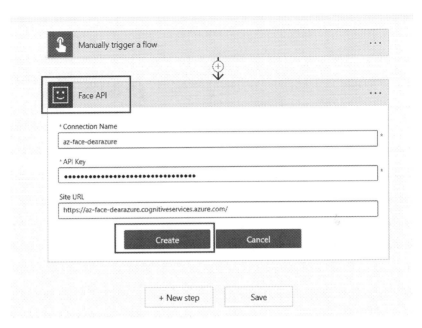

Figure 5-17. *Adding Face service connection*

These details will be used by the connector to perform the cognitive action on the data sent as input; in our case, it is a manual process, but it can be passed by any available source, such as Azure Blob storage. Once all the details are added, click Create.

Now its time to provide the image URL to this connector. To do so, click in the text box, and you will see the list of content available from the preceding step. Here, select Input from the list to provide the URL with the value passed as input (Figure 5-18).

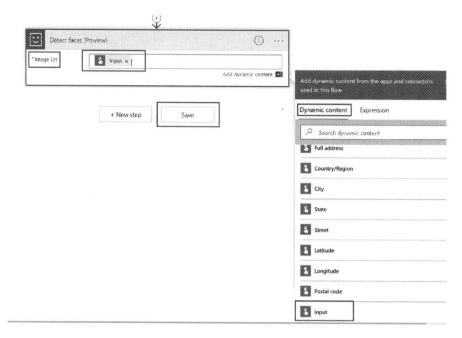

Figure 5-18. *Adding input for the Face connector*

Click Save and use Flow Checker to check for any errors or warnings. The results are shown in Figure 5-19.

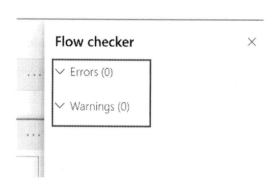

Figure 5-19. *Window presenting any errors and warnings*

Now, we are ready to trigger and test the workflow. Click Test on the right, as shown in Figure 5-20.

Figure 5-20. *Testing the workflow*

Alternately, you can click Run on the top menu.

Figure 5-21. *Running the workflow*

This will open up a blade on the top right side of the page. Here you need to enter the input text value, in our case the image URL. Once that input value is provided, the Run Flow button will be enabled, as shown in Figure 5-22.

Figure 5-22. *Run Flow blade*

The image I will be passing as the input is uploaded in my Azure blob. The image URL, shown as the Input value in Figure 5-22, is `https://blurstorageda.blob.core.windows.net/upload/face-test-image.jpg`. The image is displayed in Figure 5-23.

Figure 5-23. *Image used for testing the workflow*

Click Run Flow. On successful start of the flow, you will be presented with the message shown in Figure 5-24.

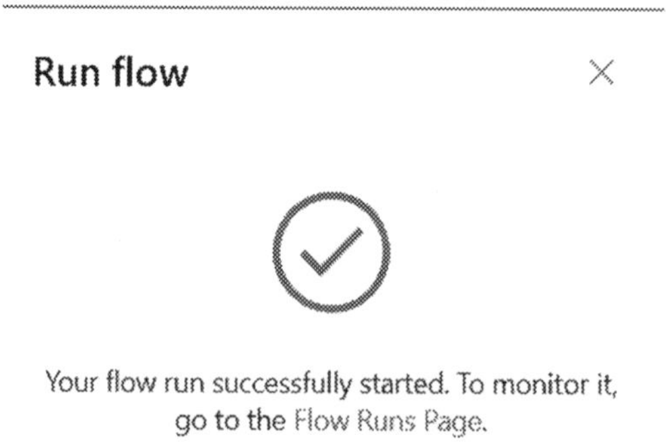

Run flow   ×

Your flow run successfully started. To monitor it, go to the Flow Runs Page.

Figure 5-24. *Confirmation that the flow is triggered*

Click the link shown in Figure 5-24 to display the output. The response and flow are displayed in Figure 5-25.

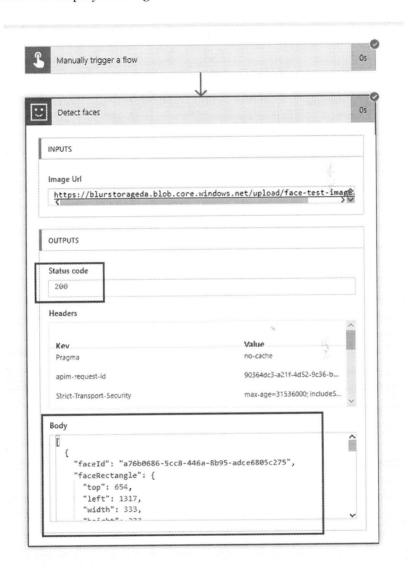

Figure 5-25. *Flow with run logs*

Let me copy and paste the response to be clearer. Figure 5-26 details the response output received from the Face connector. You can clearly see that it details the face ID with face coordinates, gender, and age, along with emotions on the face. It even mentions the subject's glasses.

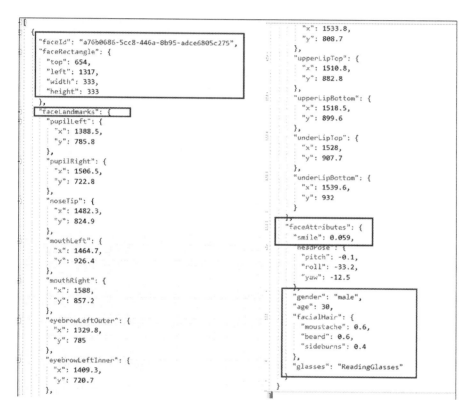

Figure 5-26. *Response recived from Face connector*

You can use this service for face recognition password functionality in business workflows, and many other use cases.

Computer Vision

As defined in Microsoft documents, "Azure's Computer Vision service provides developers with access to advanced algorithms that process images and return information based on the visual features you're interested in. For example, Computer Vision can determine whether an image contains adult content, find specific brands or objects, or find human faces."

To start, create a Computer Vision service in Azure Portal. Add a new connector for the Computer Vision service in a Power Automate workflow. Add the action name Describe Image.

The workflow will look like the illustration in Figure 5-27.

Figure 5-27. *Flow with Computer Vision connector*

Let's now run it in the same way, using a different image, as displayed in Figure 5-28.

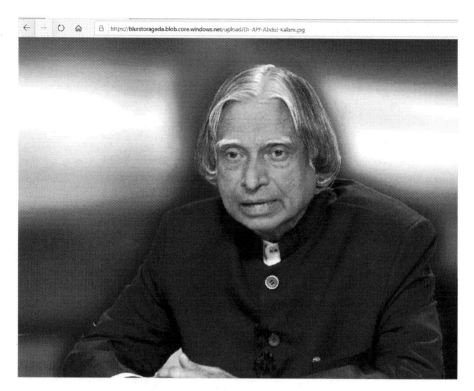

Figure 5-28. Image used to test the flow

The output is shown in Figure 5-29. Notice that it describes the image perfectly. It even recognizes the celebrity, Honourable Dr. A. P. J. Abdul Kalam, in the image. I used this image just to demonstrate the features of Computer Vision.

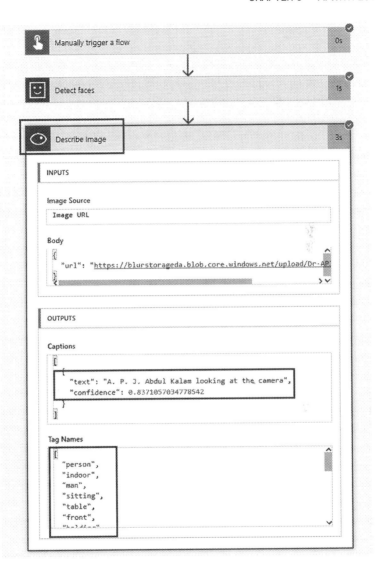

Figure 5-29. *Flow with run logs*

Text Analytics

This service enables you to detect key phrases, detect language, and detect sentiments of the given text content. The content could be anything: your company's tweet related to a product, comments on your YouTube channel, or any issues or reviews added for a product in GitHub or the SharePoint portal.

Here, I will pass a tweet containing the #aiforallbyks hashtag to the Text Analytics service and detect the sentiment of the tweet. Text Analytics returns the sentiment in the form of a score between 0 (the lowest) and 1 (the highest).

Let's create the Text Analytics service in Azure Portal.

Open Power Automate, and add Twitter as the trigger connector to collect the tweet that includes #aiforallbyks. Once someone tweets with this hashtag, our flow will be triggered, and the tweet will be passed to the Text Analytics service, which in turn detects the sentiments and returns a score.

Our workflow will look like Figure 5-30.

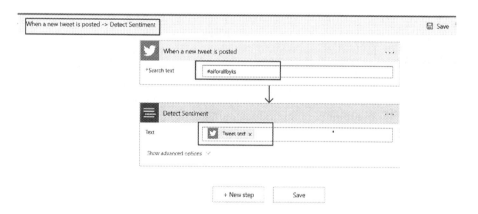

Figure 5-30. *Flow for detecting a tweet sentiment*

Now tweet a positive review with the hashtag, like the example shown in Figure 5-31, to trigger our workflow and then analyze the score returned as output from the Text Analytics – Detect Sentiment service.

Figure 5-31. *Tweet for testing*

This triggered our flow in Power Automate, and generated a score of 0.9, as highlighted in Figure 5-32.

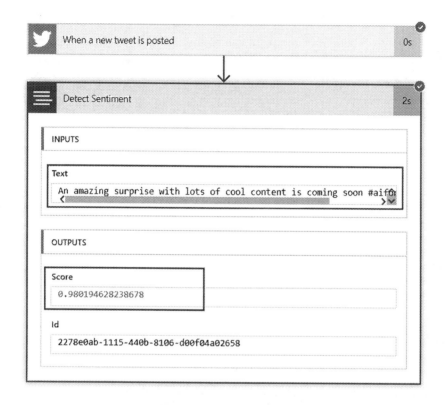

Figure 5-32. *Flow response and score*

Now, let's tweet a negative comment, like the example in Figure 5-33, to check the score.

Dear Azure | **AZ-INDIA**
@dearazure_net

No No No, cant expect such dumb content, no never.
#aiforallbyks [Test]

1:59 AM · Jun 16, 2020 · Twitter Web App

View Tweet activity

Figure 5-33. *Negative tweet for testing*

As you can see in Figure 5-34, when you check the workflow for this example, the score is 0.1.

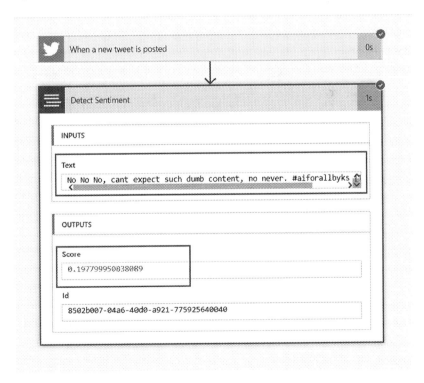

Figure 5-34. *Flow response*

You can use all the other available Azure Cognitive Services in your Power Automate workflows, along with other cognitive services as APIs or custom connectors. This can make your business workflow smarter and more intelligent with minimal to no code.

Summary

In this chapter, you learned about low-code platforms, Microsoft products as low-code platforms, and how you can leverage Azure AI services in Power Automate, a low-code product. We created a couple of workflows using this service, and also analyzed the amazing output. You should be well versed and ready to use the Azure AI services in the Azure ecosystem, be it integration, back ends, serverless, cloud search, or low-code platforms. My sole objective was to introduce and help to kickstart AI implementation in your applications hosted in and with Azure resources.

AI is meant for empowerment: to do good, to do healthy, and to do smart. Machine learning as a service and Azure AI services will definitely help you in your own empowerment journey. Try out all the demos and exercises on your own, and keep up with new announcements with respect to Azure Cognitive Services. If you have any queries or concerns, you can always reach me via LinkedIn or Twitter, and I will always be happy to help you.

Happy Azure AI learning!

Index

A

Artificial intelligence (AI), 1

Automatic tuning

  Azure SQL Database,
    enabling, 55, 56

  Azure SQL Server, enabling

    creation, 50

    database, creation, 48

    mandatory details, 49

    marketplace view, 47

    options, 53

    page, 54

    resource group, 52

    review and create tab, 51

  Azure SQL workloads, 43

  mechanism, 44

  options, 45

  recommendations, viewing

    Azure Automation
      Account, 58–64

    Azure Management Portal, 57

    PowerShell script, 63

    sent email notification, 64–68

Azure AI Services, low-code
  platform, 159, 160

Azure Automation account

  PowerShell script, 59, 61, 62

  runbook creation, 59

Azure Blob Storage, 17, 128

Azure cognitive search

  AI, 1

  creation

    Azure resource, 10

    basics tab, details, 11, 12

    ingest (*see* Ingest, Azure
      cognitive search)

    networking tab, 15

    pricing tiers, 12

    resource overview
      page, 15

    resource page, 11

    scale tab details, 12, 13

    tags tab details, 13, 14

  data formats, 3

  data sources, 3

  enrichment

    cutting-edge AI
      services, 6, 7

    data ingested, 7

    form in pattern, 6

    sample skill set, 8

  explore pattern, 9

  features, 2

  ingest pattern, 3–5

  JFK Files web app, 37

  service pattern view, 2

© Kasam Shaikh 2020
K. Shaikh, *Demystifying Azure AI*, https://doi.org/10.1007/978-1-4842-6219-1